EQUIPPING THE SAINTS TO

SERVE THE CITY

EQUIPPING THE SAINTS TO

SERVE THE CITY:

MULTICULTURAL EDUCATION FOR LAY

LEADERS' INCLUSIVE MINISTRY

by

Altagracia Pérez-Bullard

Claremont Press

Equipping the Saints to Serve the City
©2025 Claremont Press
10497 Wilshire Blvd
Los Angeles, CA 90024

ISBN 978-1-946230-65-2 (paperback)
ISBN 978-1-946230-66-9 (e-book)

Library of Congress Cataloging-in-Publication Data
Altagracia Pérez-Bullard
Equipping the Saints to Serve the City: Multicultural Education for Lay
Leaders' Inclusive Ministry

ACKNOWLEDGMENTS

This work is a communal project. My ministry and my research could not be without the Lay Ministers of the Church who have been my teachers and colleagues. The first to take me under his wings, Canon Larue Shepherd of The Episcopal Church of St. Philip the Evangelist, Los Angeles, CA was followed by too many to name both there and at The Episcopal Church of the Holy Faith, Inglewood, CA. Thank you for my formation.

I am very grateful to the Sisterhood of the Broken Toys, The Revs. Gutierrez, Janelle, Olson and Richards for sustaining me and informing this work through conversation, debate, exploration, companionship, and prayer. I am also grateful for the encouragement and support of Dean Sheryl Kujawa-Holbrook, Dean Elizabeth Conde-Frazier, and Professor Helene Slessarev-Jamir, you were right.

My family made this possible, thank you Cynthia Bullard-Pérez, my wife, and our children, Veronica, Immanuel, Josh and Jasmine, WE did it! To God be the Glory.

TABLE OF CONTENTS

PREFACE

This text is now ten years old. Since its completion I have served in two contexts that affirm this work continues to be relevant. I had the privilege of serving as the Canon for Congregational Vitality in the Diocese of New York under the Right Reverend Andrew M. L. Dietsche, the 16th Bishop of New York from 2014-2019. In 2019 I joined the faculty of Virginia Theological Seminary in Alexandria as Assistant Professor of Practical Theology. My work with students in the classroom, and as Director of Contextual Ministries (2020-2024), working with clergy and lay supervisors of students, and now as Associate Dean of Multicultural Ministries (2024), has confirmed my experience working with the lay and clergy leaders in the Diocese of New York. The changes facing congregational leaders continue to be daunting and lay people need formation and training to be responsive to the ministries to which they are called in ever more diverse contexts.

In addition to the ongoing institutional challenge of declining and aging membership due to multiple complex factors, the experience of the COVID-19 pandemic severely challenged church leaders from 2020-2022.[1] The Episcopal Church, along with all societal and community institutions, suffered from, adapted to, and is recovering from the impact of this pandemic.[2] In their observations and insights from the narrative responses to the 2022 Parochial Report, Taylor Hartson of the University of Notre Dame, identifies four major themes: returning to worship, sustaining

---

[1] For a review of the events impacting U.S. society during the height of the COVID-19 pandemic see the "CDC Museum COVID-19 Timeline," https://www.cdc.gov/museum/timeline/covid19.html, accessed November 4, 2024.

[2] Taylor Hartson, "Pandemic Paradoxes: New Patterns of Engagement in a Post-Pandemic World, Observations and Insights from Narrative Responses to the 2022 Parochial Report," Summary of 2022 Episcopal Report Comments, August 2023, https://extranet.generalconvention.org/staff/files/download/32270?_gl=1*a0f61 r*_ga*MjAzNjY4OTY4My4xNzMwNzM0NzQ2*_ga_8C0Q9J2J2F*MTczMDczNDc 0NS4xLjEuMTczMDczNDc2Ny4wLjAuMA.%20accessed%20November%204,%20 2024.

growth, recovering generations, and planning for longevity. Responses reflect a desire to sustain growth that had begun in 2022. "Though many parishes struggled to re-engage existing membership, newcomers and visitors offered an opportunity to grow and engage a new group of people."[3] Quotes from respondents point to the need for formation and discipleship as they seek to embrace the opportunity and challenge these newcomers present, and in turn the need to involve more members of the congregation in these ministries. The development of leaders who can support new and different/diverse members in their formation and engagement within congregations facing dramatic change continues to be critical. Whether in conversation with congregational leaders or students, the need for a framework and strategy to support the growth of lay leaders remains urgent.

---

[3] Hartson, "Summary of 2022 Episcopal Report Comments," p. 9.

CHAPTER ONE

Introduction

Urgent: Leaders Needed

All mainline denominations' churches are experiencing great change in the contexts they have historically served, and this context of change and increased urbanization is a worldwide phenomenon. The movement of peoples and the disruption of villages, towns, and families is a product of the forces of globalization from which none are exempt. This makes it timely and important to study those congregations that have been ministering in diverse urban contexts and have been living as multicultural communities. The parishes of St. Mary's Episcopal Church, Koreatown and Holy Faith Episcopal Church, Inglewood in the Diocese of Los Angeles have been multicultural for decades. Presenting their cases, detailing their practices, and chronicling their history through the review of documents, an analysis of their contexts, and thick description of their common life will provide important information for the fields of Practical Theology and Christian Education, as well as for the lay leadership of other congregations in similar contexts.

The development of lay leadership is essential, especially for a congregation that seeks revitalization and growth. The long-term leadership of congregations is in the hands of lay people. The church, defined as the people of God gathered in congregations, is composed mostly of lay people, with clergy leaders transitioning in and out of congregations every few years. Clergy leadership may encourage, promote, and even initiate changes in structure, power, and culture, but these cannot be sustained without the cooperation and participation of the lay people.

Congregations that seek to create multicultural, multilingual community find few resources available to support the necessary skill development and community building. Yet multicultural congregations have ministered in complex contexts. Studying the

1

case of two congregations living with complex issues of diversity will allow me to analyze the types of leadership development they use and the appropriateness of Critical Multicultural Education as a resource for leadership development in these complex urban contexts.

Holy Faith Episcopal Church, Inglewood and St. Mary's Episcopal Church, Koreatown, are both located in urban centers of the Diocese of Los Angeles where there is a great deal of cultural and economic diversity. Their membership is racially, ethnically, economically, and theologically diverse. They have both had experience conducting worship in languages other than English. They have served immigrant communities and have membership that is multigenerational. They are both interested in serving the neighbors that surround them, in communities whose populations have shifted dramatically. They seek to welcome their neighbors, and given the demographic shifts, this in turn will increase the diversity of the congregation. They wish to continue to be inclusive and diverse, and to welcome to their community others who will bring additional elements that will continue to diversify the community.

The terms "diverse" and "multicultural" are highly contested. In the field of education this has led to conflicting definitions, each reflective of different pedagogies. In the field of religious education, among those concerned with the formation of believers, some people have come to distrust the terms. Barbara Wilkerson responds by explicitly distinguishing her discussion of multiculturalism from the discussion of politics that have been controversial in educational circles.[1]

Eduardo Manuel Duarte and Stacy Smith open their edited volume, *Foundational Perspectives in Multicultural Education* by directly addressing this contestation of definitions. Conceding the ambiguity of the term, they distinguish between the multicultural condition and multiculturalisms. Their text reviews multiculturalism from a variety of perspectives and discusses issues in the ethnicity/race/culture matrix to narrow the scope of the

---

[1] Barbara Wilkerson, ed., *Multicultural Religious Education* (Birmingham, Alabama: Religious Education Press, 1997), 2-4.

investigation.[2] Others regard multiculturalism as a continuum of issues that engage the "multicultural condition," the reality of pluralism in our society. Joe L. Kincheloe and Shirley R. Steinberg, in *Changing Multiculturalism,* discuss the range of issues, from appreciation and tolerance of cultural, racial, and ethnic differences to seeking to build an inclusive society in which domination and oppression do not define the interaction between different communities.[3] Kincheloe and Steinberg argue for a critical multiculturalism that has as its pedagogical vision the development of persons prepared to engage injustice and contribute to building a democratic society that is accessible to all communities without the power imbalance caused by white privilege, patriarchy, and classism. This critical multicultural education has as its goal social justice, the starting premise that "equity and justice should be goals for everyone and that solidarity across differences is needed to bring about justice."[4]

This understanding of right relations in the human community is closest to the beloved community described in the Christian scriptures. Faith formation has always incorporated aspects of living in right relation with one's neighbor, the other, in response to Jesus naming the love of God and neighbor as the core teaching of all the prophets.[5] The church is called to work against injustice in any form. "Centrally placed within the Holy Scriptures is an indelible foundational message of God's intention for justice and peace for all humanity."[6] Congregations committed to creating just, inclusive, multicultural community seek to welcome all persons, and to engage the city and its pluralism. To practice creating radically

---

[2] Eduardo Manuel Duarte and Stacy Smith, *Foundational Perspectives in Multicultural Education* (New York: Longman, 2000), 2-3.
[3] Joe L. Kincheloe and Shirley R. Steinberg, *Changing Multiculturalism* (Buckingham: Open University Press, 1997).
[4] Christine E. Sleeter and Carl A. Grant, *Making Choices for Multicultural Education: Five Approaches to Race, Class, and Gender* (Hoboken, New Jersey: Wiley & Sons, 2009), 184.
[5] Matt. 22:37-40.
[6] Joseph Barndt, *Becoming an Anti-Racist Church: Journeying Toward Wholeness* (Minneapolis: Fortress, 2011), 11.

welcoming communities is a spiritual practice that reflects the love of God, and the call to just community.[7]

An inclusive and diverse congregation is one that is not only racially, ethnically, and linguistically diverse but also one that recognizes the diversity of persons who differ in their physical abilities, mental health, sexual/gender identity (Lesbian, Gay, Bisexual, Transgender, Queer, Intersexed, Asexual, and more or LGBTQIA+), class, and educational/professional status. I am being explicit about the last two categories because in many immigrant communities people have completed some higher education and are professionals in their countries of origin, but because of issues of immigration status are working in the United States as part of the underground economy, as domestics, nannies, housekeepers, etc. In this context there is a difference between these persons and persons who are poor and have no formal education, or are indigent. To be welcoming to these various populations, which often live in the same area as the others, given the realities of gentrification and urban renewal, is the challenge of congregations that seek to be truly multicultural and inclusive.

Given this definition of diversity it is clear that diversity is a part of all congregational life, not just of congregations in the urban, pluralistic core. Many congregations may at first glance seem homogenous, but they too encompass diversity. This intersection of identities is present in all communities (given the cultural aspects of race, ethnicities, class, etc.). Studying these bounded cases through the lens of critical multicultural education will provide the opportunity to apply the framework and strategies of this pedagogical stance and praxis to the development of lay leaders in multicultural congregations seeking to be inclusive and welcoming in their diverse contexts, but will also provide insight for more "traditional" and "homogenous" congregations.

Experiential Context

I am excited at the prospect of learning in a systematic way from these two bounded cases. The materials available on leadership formation do not address the complex contexts of urban

---

[7] Stephanie Spellers, *Radical Welcome: Embracing God, The Other, and the Spirit of Transformation* (New York: Church Publishing, 2006), 6.

multicultural congregations. In my twenty-three years of congregational leadership I have been frustrated with the lack of adequate formation tools. It was through asking colleagues about the strategies that they were implementing in a similar context, about what they were learning through that process, and about how they were adapting and applying available resources, that I learned and applied what was needed in a challenging ministry. For congregational leaders, especially lay leaders, it is helpful to have learning communities where they can ask questions, share experiences, and design strategies. How can congregational leaders understand the interconnectedness of the various issues that impact urban communities and the ways that they impact community building both within and without the church? What are the praxis models, frameworks, and strategies that can be brought to bear in this context? It is hard work to review and adapt materials prepared for other contexts, translating materials only available in English, and learning through trial and error the best way to initiate difficult conversations. I have been impressed by the commitment of congregational leadership to live their call to be an inclusive multicultural community even when it has meant change and turnover. I have been impressed by the willingness of members, especially the lay leaders/vestry (church board) members, to listen carefully to one another, to be challenged and learn new ways of working together, and to risk doing something different in the hope of getting a different result. It is important for the health of the broader church to share the knowledge gained by congregations engaged in this work. Issues of globalization, pluralism, and increased urbanization impact all congregations in all communities. Learning from these bounded cases will facilitate the process for other congregations, not because there would be a structured program to be implemented, but because these cases provide material for reflection and discussion as congregations analyze their own contexts and engage in life-giving praxis.

Critical multicultural education's commitment to social justice is central to its appropriateness as a resource for urban inclusive congregations.[8] Such justice-centered pedagogy gives people the opportunity to learn about difference from each other and from

---

[8] Kincheloe and Steinberg, *Changing Multiculturalism*, 26.

reflection on their shared praxis, and to practice empathy.[9] This study will explore the use of these liberative pedagogies in the development of leadership, and their appropriateness to the complex contexts of these cases.

This study analyzes these cases from a critical theory perspective, assessing the impact of issues of race, class, gender, sexual orientation, and disability on a diverse congregation. The review and analysis from this perspective is in keeping with the justice work in which these congregations have been involved, seeking to welcome and serve those in their community, especially those in need. The study also reviews and analyzes literature on urban ministry, and critical multicultural education in an effort to identify, through the use of the case studies, their applicability to leadership development for these bounded cases.

Context of and Justification for Study

In the preface to Lovett H. Weems' *Church Leadership: Vision Team, Culture and Integrity,* Rosabeth Moss Kanter says, "(t)he task of leadership is change. Leaders inspire others to their best efforts in order to do better, to attain higher purposes."[10] Effective lay leaders are responsive to the changing context they are called to serve. Without a vision of a new way of being, churches will suffer from their resistance to the buffeting of constant change that is the reality of urban centers. How does church leadership facilitate a congregation to see, receive, and live into that new vision?

The aim of this qualitative research project is to analyze two case studies of urban, multicultural congregations that are seeking to be inclusive and to serve their communities. These congregations have made the effort to welcome people of various cultural backgrounds, enriching an already diverse community. What type of training is best suited for leaders who seek to do this ministry? What do the leaders need in order to be equipped to live into the challenges of an inclusive, multicultural church? How can they become increasingly diverse and culturally complex without the tools necessary for engagement, reflection, and analysis of the dynamics of diversity

---

[9] Kincheloe and Steinberg, *Changing Multiculturalism,* 43.
[10] Lovett H. Weems, Jr., *Church Leadership: Vision, Team, Culture and Integrity* (Nashville: Abingdon, 1993), 11.

amongst themselves in order to be better able to welcome the "other?" Utilizing the bounded cases of two urban, multicultural, Episcopal parishes in the Diocese of Los Angeles, I will analyze the issues facing the lay leadership, and assess the appropriateness of applying Critical Multicultural Education theory and praxis as a model for leadership development that seeks to be responsive to this fluid and challenging context.

Equipping congregational leaders to manage change, cultural diversity, population shifts, limited resources, and a range of theological beliefs has been the focus of my full-time parish ministry for the past twenty years. In that time, I have found few resources that equip church leaders to lead in contexts of change and diversity or that address the needs of urban congregations seeking to be responsive to their communities' ever-changing needs. Many congregations in need of revitalization after great shifts in the community population have sought to invite their new and always culturally different neighbors to join them in doing church as they have always done it. In some instances, they have established separate worship services for these new neighbors, thereby minimizing disturbance of the status quo. These churches have met with limited success. Yet they reflect the church growth perspective that says that interracial and multicultural churches cannot be sustained. The common wisdom is that churches need to identify a target population that they will serve and then design church programs and worship to serve that community with its particular cultural and socioeconomic realities.[11] Urban churches that are integrated are seen as churches in transition from serving one community to serving another and are not thought to be sustainable.

Congregations with a new vision of what it means to be church in the urban core are challenging the belief that multicultural, multiracial, multiethnic congregations cannot be sustained. In *Urban Church Education*, the authors present an alternative to the market-segmenting model of church growth, and the development of the laity is central to the strategy of church growth and revitalization.[12] The church is called to be what it teaches: a community that reflects

---

[11] Walter E. Ziegenhals, *Urban Churches in Transition* (New York: Pilgrim, 1978), 102.

[12] Donald B. Rogers, ed., *Urban Church Education* (Birmingham: Religious Education Press, 1989).

God's inclusive love and justice.[13] The churches at these early stages of integration see their diversity as a gift to be celebrated, without recognizing and addressing the challenges that are presented by the different cultural perspectives and lived realities. The dominant culture of mainline Protestantism is taken as a given, as normative. The invitation to the new neighbors is typically to come join us as we are and be with us as we are accustomed. Issues of race, class, gender, sexual orientation, theological difference, and physical and mental (dis)ability are seen as divisive and a threat to the community.

In *A Many Colored Kingdom, Multicultural Dynamics for Spiritual Formation*,[14] the authors address this tendency to avoid the real consequences of diversity and the issues of power that must be addressed if diverse communities are to live justly. They identify and outline educational theories and theological frameworks that foster an understanding of the power dynamics inherent in multicultural contexts. This delineation will inform the work of this present study, which will take it a step further. What are the questions and strategies that must be engaged in order to foster congregational leadership that can be responsive to the urban context? How does one address the discomfort inherent in these discussions so that people are empowered not only to engage injustice but also to reflect in their relationships the values of love, justice, and mercy that are the gospel imperatives?

An important aspect of the education and reflection for these congregations will be learning about the hegemony of whiteness. Like many mainline denominations in the United States the culture of the Episcopal Church is European. The ties to the Church of England are continuous and what is identified as Episcopal worship and polity is culturally English. This is true not only of White churches in the United States, but also of immigrant churches that serve Anglicans from the former British colonies. The understanding of these colonial churches with regards to worship and church practices are culturally European. Understanding "whiteness" then becomes important in unpacking the cultural

---

[13] Rogers, *Urban Church Education*, 85.
[14] Elizabeth Conde-Frazier, S. Steve Kang, and Gary A. Parrett, *A Many Colored Kingdom: Multicultural Dynamics for Spiritual Formation* (Grand Rapids: Baker Academic), 2004.

identity of Episcopalians, and in some ways is more difficult in congregations with many people of color from the former colonies. In order to incorporate the many cultures and histories of the people who attend these churches there must be a discussion about the cultural assumptions that define how the community functions, and how these assumptions can be challenged in order to welcome other cultural assumptions that are shared by the members of the church and the surrounding community yet are not traditionally thought of as "Episcopalian."

It is this level of critical reflection and learning that suggests that Critical Multicultural Education is the appropriate framework of diversity education indicated in this context. In *Changing Multiculturalism*, Kincheloe and Steinberg discuss the many ways that the term multiculturalism has been used in educational contexts. The term multiculturalism incorporates various categories of diversity: "race, socio-economic class, gender, language, culture, sexual preference or disability."[15] Kincheloe and Steinberg present a "democratic multiculturalism concerned with social justice and community building."[16] Their understanding of multiculturalism addresses head-on the critique offered by Peter J. McLaren, in which he indicts the practice of many multiculturalists of relativizing oppression as "subjective feeling," "reduced to communicative practices removed from larger social and economic structures of domination."[17] He sees a lack of acknowledgement of the complexity created by the intersection of diversity, power, and privilege: "There appears to be a general lack of awareness that race, class, gender and sexuality are non-synchronous and crisscrossed by vectors of privilege and relations of inequality."[18] Where he continues the analysis with an emphasis on the materiality of forces, and the realities of state power and economic structures, this critique of many multiculturalists is quite applicable to the church and its structures and practices. The celebration of cultural practices (clothing, food, music, dance, and even liturgical acts) is not sufficient if the goal is the creation of an inclusive multicultural

---

[15] Kincheloe and Steinberg, *Changing Multiculturalism*, 1.
[16] Kincheloe and Steinberg, *Changing Multiculturalism*, 2.
[17] Kincheloe and Steinberg, *Changing Multiculturalism*, viii.
[18] Kincheloe and Steinberg, *Changing Multiculturalism*, viii.

community committed to justice. Issues of oppression, power and privilege must be addressed in order to create a just community.

This reality, which this study explores in the development of the bounded cases, indicates the appropriateness of the use of Critical Multicultural Education as a way of learning about diversity and the issues of power and oppression that are inherent in churches formed through missionary activity associated with imperial colonialism. Reviewing and analyzing both the congregational leadership materials, contexts, and particular histories of these congregations and the literature on critical multicultural education allows me to offer this study as a possible resource not only for these two congregations but also for other urban multicultural congregations that seek to be diverse and inclusive.

Methodology and Contribution to the Field of Practical Theology and the Discipline of Christian Education

To support churches that seek to live out the gospel imperatives in their congregational life is the work of practical theology. Such theology "seeks to explore the complex dynamics of particular situations in order to enable the development of a transformative and illuminating understanding of what is going on within these situations."[19] Practical theology as a field of study in the academy is concerned with the practices of people of faith. It has a "vital orientation to faithful ways of living in and for the world."[20] As practical theologians reflect on the ways that people and communities practice their faith in God by living attuned to God's mercy and justice, they offer to the church and its leadership an essential service.

The work of Christian Education within this field of study is to provide opportunities and resources for the healthy development of believers' life of faith. In some of the best models of urban multicultural ministry this means that Christian formation is the primary work of the church and should be reflected in all areas of

---

[19] John Swinton and Harriet Mowat, *Practical Theology and Qualitative Research* (London: SCM Press, 2009), v.
[20] Dorothy C. Bass and Craig Dykstra, eds., *For Life Abundant: Practical Theology, Theological Education and Christian Ministry* (Grand Rapids: William B. Eerdmans, 2008), 4.

church life. "The significance and power of the teaching ministry in center-city churches is illustrated in nearly every congregation described in this volume. The power and attractiveness of good teaching begins with the sermon and extends throughout the total program."[21] This "faith community approach to Christian formation"[22] most accurately describes how formation happens, "learning the faith happens as the members of a faith community participate, intentionally and unintentionally, in the activities of that community."[23] Therefore, formation, training, and education, both intentional and indirect, occur in the life of the community. Studying the bounded cases of these communities and their practices will show how they have developed their lay leaders and how critical multicultural education can address the gaps in their formation. The complexity of oppressive systems in urban contexts requires intentional lay leadership development. Critical Multicultural Education best equips lay leaders for relevant and transformative ministry within these urban contexts.

---

[21] Lyle E. Schaller, ed., *Center City Churches: The New Urban Frontier* (Nashville: Abingdon, 1993), 12.

[22] Conde-Frazier, Kang, and Parrett, *A Many Colored Kingdom*, 80.

[23] Conde-Frazier, Kang, and Parrett, *A Many Colored Kingdom*, 80.

CHAPTER TWO

Literature Survey

Why are there bodies in the river? Developing ministry that transforms the context. Lay leaders are the long-term ministers in churches, yet their leadership development has not been explored in the literature, and the urban center as a context has not been fully analyzed, nor its oppressive structures that need to be dismantled.

Urbanization is rising rapidly. Globalization increases migration from rural areas to urban ones, from cities in poorer nations, to cities in richer nations. Ministry in these contexts is increasingly complex. In the United States, these forces impact the mission of churches traditionally designed to serve a rural context and is being felt in cities around the world.[1] Equipping church leadership to respond effectively to this complex and changing ministerial context is a challenge that has not been addressed directly. Diversity calls for new paradigms of ministry in order to welcome and engage people whose life experience is different from that of most mainline dominant culture protestant congregations. Welcoming as equals, people identified as minorities with all the realities that this label brings, issues of power, justice, domination and oppression, requires training leaders for dealing with these issues.

The literature on church leadership development has focused on the role of professional clergy. Yet the biblical model of church leadership is one of shared leadership, where all the baptized, are called to minister to the world in Christ's name. [2] This literature survey reviews published texts on the topic of urban ministry to find

---

[1] For a useful discussion of this phenomenon see Raymond J. Bakke and Jim Hart, "The Lord is Shaking Up the World," in *The Urban Christian: Effective Ministry in Today's Urban World* (Downers Grove: InterVarsity Press, 1987), chapter 2.
[2] The Urban Bishops Coalition, *To Hear and to Heed: The Episcopal Church Listens and Acts in the City* (Cincinnati: Forward Movement Publications, 1978), 4.

material on the development of lay leadership for urban multicultural ministry. The working assumption of this literature survey is that lay leadership is in need of formation and development to deal with great changes and transitions in urban communities, and to respond effectively, together with clergy, to the challenges of multicultural congregations.

Upon completion of this initial survey I will briefly review literature that utilizes a social justice lens to equip congregational leaders for ministry. Although always an important ministerial component, social justice ministries are especially central in congregations where issues of urban decline, poverty and discrimination impact the community's quality of life. Congregational leaders need practices and strategies that support their work of visioning and ministering to communities in transition. Literature in this vein responds to ministerial needs that assume that learning for ministry in these contexts is most effective when action-reflection is the pedagogical model. Therefore many of the texts provide case studies that share the experience and learning of other congregational leaders doing ministry in similar contexts.

The survey will show that there are several resources that address issues of urban churches, leadership development, social justice ministries, and diversity. They emphasize either issues of culture, or race, or the methodology of action-reflection, but they do not focus on the ways that these intersect and the interplay of these issues and methodology. I believe that this is where application of critical multicultural education methodologies can bring together the interdisciplinary tools and perspectives to address the complex and multilayered nature of oppression that impacts urban churches and communities.

This survey identifies many books written by leaders and scholars of many different denominations that address the topic of ministry in the urban context. They fall roughly into the following categories: books that serve as a general overview of urban ministry; books that offer tools for study and analysis of the church and its changing context; case studies; and books on education and formation in the urban church. This last category is the most clearly responsive to the question of urban lay ministry development, but the other materials also reflect on leadership and on lay leadership in particular.

Historical Perspective on Urban Churches

Kloetzli and Hillman offer a useful set of distinctions between the types of congregations that can be found in the metropolitan area. When the term urban ministry is used there are assumptions about great challenges and few resources to respond to them, poor education, poor health outcomes and poor economic opportunities. This is often the case. However, with urban renewal and gentrification along with the phenomenon of the mega church, this assumption does not apply in every case. **The downtown church** is usually the first established by the denomination in a particular community, known as the First Church or the mother church.[3] **The multi neighborhood or regional church** is located in the inner city facing the heterogeneous population with less income than the former residents.[4] **The neighborhood church** is identified with its local neighborhood; it is involved in working to improve its community, both the church and the neighborhood are relatively homogenous.[5] **The selective or special-group church** ministers to a particular subset of the population either by choice or by circumstance of history. The characteristics that identify the congregation might be race, nationality, class, or other factors, and these congregations resist change even when the community becomes more heterogeneous.[6] **The suburban church** can either be identified as being part of the older blue-collar towns that developed immediately adjacent to the metropolitan center and underwent many of the same changes as the urban core, or newer developments that are bedroom communities which are more homogeneous.[7] **The storefront church** is found in more blighted and transitional communities, is small and ministers primarily to new migrants from the rural area, and now more with immigrant communities.[8]

These characterizations are useful for both congregations and for those who study them. As issues of transition and decline impact churches and are the focus of both local and denominational leaders,

---

[3] Walter Kloetzli and Arthur Hillman, *Urban Church Planning: The Church Discovers its Community* (Philadelphia: Muhlenberg, 1958), 36-37.
[4] Kloetzli and Hillman, *Urban Church Planning*, 38-39.
[5] Kloetzli and Hillman, *Urban Church Planning*, 39-40.
[6] Kloetzli and Hillman, *Urban Church Planning*, 40-41.
[7] Kloetzli and Hillman, *Urban Church Planning*, 41-42.
[8] Kloetzli and Hillman, *Urban Church Planning*, 42-43.

these classifications demystify the reality of urban congregations. Many church leaders, feeling overwhelmed by the complexity of the difficulties they face, struggle to keep perspective on the sociological reality they share with congregations in cities everywhere. A broader and deeper recognition of the social forces that affect churches as institutions can impact strategies employed for sustainability growth and revitalization. Fully understanding the nature of the problem is critical to addressing it. These distinctions should also be taken into account when designing and adapting materials to train urban lay leaders.

Also useful in the study of urban churches is the historical survey offered by Clifford J. Green. It presents a fifty-year history useful for those responsible for planning for congregations from a denominational institutions perspective.[9] It also fills in some of the gaps that are found in the literature on urban ministry. The gaps in literature reflect the waves of attention to both issues of urban decay and development and the focus on issues of race and culture. These issues receive more consistent attention in the literature on secular education. Therefore, although dated, I will list briefly the contribution of older books on urban ministry to the development of lay leadership.

Cities and Churches: Readings on the Urban Church includes some biblical, historical and theological contexts for the work of urban ministry in the church. It uses socio cultural, economic, and psychological frameworks to present central themes in urban ministry: church renewal in the inner-city, charismatic religious groups responsive to the need of new arrivals in the city, challenges of institutional organization and roles in the face of the new reality, the church's involvement in issues of conflict and oppression, and collaboration between churches and community organizations working for improved quality of life for those in the city.[10] David W. Barry identifies as crucial the need for indigenous leadership. Identification and development of leadership is the priority of urban ministry.[11] George W. Webber offers the East Harlem Protestant Parish, a collaborative ministry in New York City as a case study

---

[9] Clifford J. Green, ed., *Churches, Cities, and Human Community: Urban Ministry in the United States, 1945-1985* (Grand Rapids: Wm. B. Eerdmans, 1996).

[10] Robert Lee, ed., *Cities and Churches: Readings on the Urban Church* (Philadelphia: Westminster, 1962).

[11] Lee, *Cities and Churches*, 145-8.

that highlights lay leadership as central to all aspects of ministry. No details are offered on the development and training of these lay leaders but the importance of their role is clear. [12]

Raymond J. Bakke and Jim Hart's overview of urban ministry provides case studies with theological reflections, in the context of global urbanization. The case studies present various effective strategies for essential leadership development, especially of lay leadership development. [13] The development takes different forms and is deployed in various contexts but lay people are central and the end of the text offers a checklist for those engaged in this work.[14] The volume edited by Wayne Stumme presents the work of urban ministry in the Lutheran church; *The Experience of Hope, Mission and Ministry in Changing Urban Communities* incorporates discussions of lay ministries as part of evangelism. These lay ministries take various forms but include service/community organizing and art projects.[15] The text discusses the role of lay leadership in general throughout the text although it never addresses it specifically. *Envisioning the New City* presents a new vision for urban ministry for the education of leaders, worship, community building and organizing and public policy, and was the result of a gathering of urban missioners and professors committed to the cities.[16] The essays in *Discipling the City* seek to combine the call to proclaim the gospel with the tools of research and social analysis for greater effectiveness. It is addressed to students preparing for urban ministry and is a resource for leadership development.[17]

Case Studies and Success Stories

There are many books that present models and lessons learned from those engaged in urban ministry. Michael J. Christensen's *City Streets City People: A Call for Compassion*[18] presents the story of his

---

[12] Lee, *Cities and Churches*, 167-9.

[13] Bakke and Hart, *The Urban Christian*, chapter 2.

[14] Bakke and Hart, *The Urban Christian*, 188.

[15] Wayne Stumme, ed., *The Experience of Hope: Mission and Ministry in Changing Urban Communities* (Minneapolis: Augsburg, 1991).

[16] Eleanor Scott Meyers, ed., *Envisioning the New City: A Reader on Urban Ministry* (Louisville: Westminster/John Knox, 1992), 19-20.

[17] Roger S. Greenway, ed., *Discipling the City: A Comprehensive Approach to Urban Ministry* (Eugene: Wipf & Stock, 1997).

[18] Michael J. Christensen, *City Streets City People: A Call for Compassion* (Nashville: Abingdon, 1988).

journey with an intentional Christian community that served in a poor community in San Francisco. It offers the experience of this community as a model of development of lay people for ministry. *Center City Churches: The New Urban Frontier* presents case studies of center city churches, specifically large, successful urban ministries. Church leaders witness to the work of their church in the urban center, sharing best practices and the process by which programs and ministries were developed, including several examples of lay leader training and development models for ministry in the congregation and in the community.[19]

A very different, yet also concrete approach to congregational development for ministry appears in Philip Amerson's *Tell Me City Stories: A Journey for Urban Congregations*.[20] This book uses a narrative approach to research the congregation and the community for ministry development. The book is a manual that articulates the powerful role that sharing stories and experiences can have for gathering the vision of the community, identifying the needs and the gifts of the community, and developing strategies for ministries.

The manual presents stories on the various themes of urban ministry development with case studies of congregations going through this process. It offers instructions to bring the congregation through the same process, along with exercises and discussion questions. Discussions include topics of visioning, internal congregational dynamics, community needs, cultural differences, and the challenges they present as well as strategies for ministry development. It is set up as a journey, and in the end, the purpose is to do asset based planning, that is, to highlight the gifts of being a faith community in the city, in response to the challenges that many congregations experience in difficult transitional communities.

Urban Christian Education for Leadership Development

The issue of urban communities in transition, especially racial transition, produced material to educate and inform church leaders about what they were facing. This typically included information about the socio-economic, cultural, and social psychological dynamics that have implications for the ministry of the church.

---

[19] Schaller, *Center City Churches*.

[20] Philip Amerson, *Tell Me City Stories: A Journey for Urban Congregations* (Eugene: Wipf & Stock, 2003).

Urban Churches in Transition by Walter E. Ziegenhals presents a detailed analysis of the situation facing communities in the process of racial transition.[21] Following that are two specific case studies of churches in transition. Ziegenhals identifies the importance of competent and creative clergy leadership for working in a difficult transitional setting, and also the difficulty in identifying and retaining such leadership, especially black leadership, in the long term in difficult situations.[22] Black clerical leadership is important because Ziegenhals does not believe in the sustainability of an interracial congregation. Mixed communities can only be sustained while the community remains mixed; if the transition completely changes the community, the congregation will not be able to maintain its mixed character.[23] Congregations that seek to live intentionally as multicultural communities, challenge this assumption about congregational development. This model is not only possible but given the gospel imperatives it is essential for the church as it seeks to live into its calling in a pluralistic society.

The essays compiled in *Urban Church Education* directly address the question of training and development of the laity for urban ministry. Therefore, although dated, it bears reviewing. Donald B. Rogers seeks to identify the principles of urban church education that can inform all educational programs and activities in urban churches. The principles could serve as a base for the development of indigenous educational materials and pedagogies. Theory would be in service of practice and would allow for the flexibility necessary for adjustments in the varying contexts.[24] The principles that impact the practice of urban religious education are listed at the conclusion of the essay.[25] What follows is a review of essays that focus on multicultural lay ministry development.

Letty M. Russell presents various models for religious education in an urban church, based primarily on understanding that the entire church is involved and committed to the task of educating the congregation.[26] She tackles the challenge of developing teachers by

---

[21] Ziegenhals, *Urban Churches in Transition*.
[22] Ziegenhals, *Urban Churches in Transition*, 18.
[23] Ziegenhals, *Urban Churches in Transition*, 102.
[24] Rogers, *Urban Church Education*, chapter 2.
[25] Rogers, *Urban Church Education*, 24.
[26] Letty M. Russell, "Christian Religious Education and the Inner City," in *Urban Church Education*, 30.

using a peer approach in which adults can gradually learn from lead teachers the process of planning and coaching children to assist each other in learning activities.[27] Kay Kupper Berg tackles the essentials of developing a core curriculum for Christian literacy.[28] Colleen Birchett presents the challenges of developing education programs for the black church.[29] She concludes that the Black church is now ready to focus on religious education outside of the historical context of the preaching event.[30] Captolia D. Newbern discusses the importance of leadership development for all God's people and the task of disciple making that is at the core of the church's mission. [31] "Education is the prime factor in leadership and development."[32] Although she focuses primarily on the context of the Black church, she also discusses the importance of the inclusive church as an incarnation of the will of God.[33] The opportunity for all believers to come together in worship and service to God and develop and offer their gifts in ministry is the gift of the inclusive church.[34] Bill Gambrell shares what he has learned in his congregation about church growth through adult religious education. He presents the purpose and agenda of teacher training along with the organizational method utilized by First Baptist Church of Jackson, Mississippi.[35] Richard L. Stackpole and Ron Robotham describe camping programs along with suggestions for the training of counselors.[36] Donald B. Rogers concludes with major dimensions of educating the whole congregation for mission.[37] He also suggests

---

[27] Russell, "Christian Religious Education," 37-38.

[28] Kay Kupper Berg, "Christian Literacy, the Core Curriculum, and the Urban Church, in *Urban Church Education*, 50-59.

[29] Colleen Birchett, "A History of Religious Education in the Black Church," in *Urban Church Education*, 71-83.

[30] Birchett, "A History of Religious Education," 82.

[31] Captolia D. Newbern, "Making the Dream Come True: Discipleship for All God's People in the Urban Church, in *Urban Church Education*, 102-113.

[32] Newbern, "Making the Dream Come True," 110.

[33] Newbern, "Making the Dream Come True," 112.

[34] Newbern, "Making the Dream Come True," 111.

[35] Bill Gambrell, "Urban Church Growth Through Adult Religious Education," in *Urban Church Education*, 135-141.

[36] Richard L. Stackpole and Ron Robothom, "Out of the City/Into the City: Two Camping Models for the Urban Church: Action Planning the Urban Camping Excursion, in *Urban Church Education*, 168.

[37] Rogers, "Other Models for Urban Church Education (Briefly Noted)," in *Urban Church Education*, 185.

particular points to keep in mind when educating Hispanic adults: integrating their experiences and evolving culture, the need to explore creative methods of communication, and flexibility in schedules and physical arrangements. It is necessary to take its complexities into account when evaluating the effectiveness of religious education with this population, since it is still in the early stages of development.[38]

Robert E. Jones essay speaks directly to the lessons taught by diverse, urban churches. The church is called to be what it teaches: a community that reflects God's inclusive love and justice.[39] He argues directly against the claim made by Ziegenhals and others that the multicultural, multiracial church is not viable.[40] Social homogeneity is not necessary for church viability, he says, but it is important that there be agreement among the members of the diverse groups that they will work together to improve the community, share a common interest in social justice issues, and an ability to celebrate the pluralism of the church.[41] Using the case study of the congregation, he takes the reader through a how to checklist for creating a multicultural and multiracial congregation.[42] He specifically notes education and lay and clergy leadership identification and development as important components for the development of this type of congregation. Creating this kind of community means learning about fear, how to deal with conflict, and how to get a "buy in" from the membership. The article presents a model and principles that can guide others in the development of lay leadership for a diverse urban education.

In his reflections on urban ministry, Eldin Villafañe provides a useful perspective on the issue of leadership development.[43] What is important, for this current survey, is that when he speaks of the church doing ministry he is always talking about pastoral and lay leadership doing ministry.[44] The text then provides a description of urban ministry, highlighting the elements that lead to a successful

[38] Rogers, "Other Models," 191-2.
[39] Robert E. Jones, "Learning to Face Diversity in Urban Churches," in *Urban Church Education*, 85.
[40] Jones, "Learning to Face Diversity," 87.
[41] Jones, "Learning to Face Diversity," 89-90.
[42] Jones, "Learning to Face Diversity," 93-100.
[43] Eldin Villafañe, *Seek the Peace of the City: Reflections on Urban Ministry* (Grand Rapids: William B. Eerdmans, 1995), 1.
[44] Villafañe, *Seek the Peace of the City*, 12.

ministry, especially working with Hispanics, which are summarized as an agenda for the 1990s.[45]

Part three of his book is dedicated to Urban Theological Education. Here he tackles the necessary elements for a program that will equip leadership for ministry in urban communities. Again the target of this education is both clergy and lay. Although educational tracks could be different, Villafañe sees it as important that it be sufficiently flexible so as to allow for interaction and joint work on ministry projects between clergy and laity.[46] The purposes of theological education should include: learning about pluralism and the complexities of the city; fostering reflection on theological concepts as they relate to practical ministry while developing spiritually; learning strategies to respond to the urban context that takes into account the participants' level of knowledge and experience; developing ministerial skills with the various populations in the urban context.[47] The curriculum presented takes into account the experience level of the participants, understanding that they come with a wealth of ministry experience even if they have not had formal theological education.[48] The program Villafañe develops is also designed to deal with the schedules of working people, for whom ministry is something done part time outside of their primary employment.[49] Among the courses offered in his proposal "Leadership in Ministry" is one to work with the vocational development of the participants. This model is discussed in earlier works, but the integration makes the model multilayered, holistic, and responsive to the resources that exist for ministry in the urban context.

The contributions of Agosto[50] and Jackson[51] make connections between the early church's understanding of leadership development and the essential characteristics of theological education for ministry in the city. Agosto's treatment of Paul's leadership discussion serves to begin a theology of leadership.

---

[45] Villafañe, *Seek the Peace of the City,* 73.
[46] Villafañe, *Seek the Peace of the City,* 79.
[47] Villafañe, *Seek the Peace of the City,* 84-85.
[48] Villafañe, *Seek the Peace of the City,* 85.
[49] Villafañe, *Seek the Peace of the City,* 87.
[50] Efrain Agosto, "Paul, Leadership, and the Hispanic Church," in Villafañe, *Seek the Peace of the City,* chapter 10.
[51] Bruce W. Jackson, "Urban Theological Education for Church Leadership," in Villafañe, *Seek the Peace of the City,* chapter 11.

Jackson offers a new paradigm for theological education, one that is characterized by "(1) contextualization; (2) praxis-focused ministry; (3) grounded in the present, looking to the future; and (4) servant leadership."[52] This paradigm welcomes experienced church leaders who are in the trenches to benefit from theological education while being honored for their experience. Jackson emphasizes both mentoring and applying theological material to lived experience. He identifies servant leadership as characteristic of the education process itself, not just the ministers in the field. The theological education program seeks to serve the ministers who are in turn called to serve the city. Again this approach is welcoming of the gifts of all the members of the church. It can enrich the pastors and lay leaders call to minister to the city, and also enrich traditional theological education, better equipping it to serve the church.

Religious Education as Formation for Social Engagement

Religious education, as with education in general, is a process that prepares people for living in community. Every believer is expected to participate in religious and spiritual formation to become a disciple of Jesus Christ, and to participate in the task of discipling others. The process involves and impacts the whole person. The church, both the members of the body and the community, are about formation, or in Maria Harris's words, "the church is an educational program."[53]

In *Fashion Me a People: Curriculum in the Church*, Maria Harris makes clear that the work of formation and education is the central activity of the church and it is a lifelong process for the people of God.[54] It is a process of forming agents of change in the public sphere. She concurs with Thomas Groome that education is public and political and is about the work of justice.[55] She then shows how each ministry of the church, *kerygma* (proclaiming the word), *didache* (teaching), *liturgia* (prayer and breaking bread), *koinonia* (community), and *diakonia* (caring for the needy) forms believers.[56]

---

[52] Jackson, "Urban Theological Education," 123.
[53] Maria Harris, *Fashion Me a People: Curriculum in the Church* (Louisville: Westminster John Knox, 1989), 47.
[54] Harris, *Fashion Me a People*, 38.
[55] Harris, *Fashion Me a People*, 45.
[56] Harris, *Fashion Me a People*, 16.

Religious education is essential for forming leaders to minister, serve, and participate in the transformation of their communities.

Thomas Groome's work in Christian Education also emphasizes liberative themes as central to the formation of Christian identity.[57] His text *Christian Religious Education* comprehensively addresses the practice and art of Christian Education. He summarizes in one paragraph the principles that are operative in his understanding of the field, namely,[58] to "re-create its social and ecclesial context," and to be an "education that is just and emancipatory, promoting critical consciousness, ongoing conversion, and agency for social transformation."[59] Believers are encouraged to name and share their own lived experience and the narratives/stories and vision out of which they live. This he then brings into dialogue with the Christian story and vision. This dialectical engagement leads to a re-forming of one's own life practices in light of the imperatives of the Gospel story.[60] Groome describes his approach as a five-part movement through which people of faith engage in action-reflection, or as described by other scholars, the Pastoral Reflection Cycle, or the see-judge-act reflection method.[61]

In her text *Teaching from the Heart: Theology and Educational Method*, Moore's multidisciplinary approach brings together two dominant strands in the field of religious education: theology and education. Her methodologies are especially useful to the tasks of leadership development for inclusive communities in the urban core. As a practical theologian she seeks to bring "the theory and practice of theology into dialogue with the theory and practice of

---

[57] Thomas H. Groome, *Christian Religious Education: Sharing Our Story and Vision* (San Francisco: Harper Collins, 1981).

[58] Groome, *Christian Religious Education,* x.

[59] Groome, *Christian Religious Education,* x.

[60] Thomas H. Groome, *Sharing Faith: A Comprehensive Approach to Religious Education and Pastoral Ministry: The Way of Shared Praxis* (San Francisco: HarperCollins, 1991), 135.

[61] Widely used in pastoral reflection, the see-judge-act reflection circle was first articulated as such by Cardinal Joseph Cardijn, founder of the Young Christian Worker movement, and became a critical part of the Roman Catholic Church's methodology for applying Catholic Social Teaching, presented by Pope John XXII in his encyclical *Mater et Magistra* published on 15 May 1961. "Cardijn Taught the Church to See, Judge, Act," *UCA News,* accessed October 1, 2014, http://www.ucanews.com/news/cardijn-taught-the-church-to-see-judge-act/17650.

education."[62] She brings Process theology into conversation with five pedagogies, seeking a more organic methodology for the practice of education, which has always been part and parcel of the work of theology and informed by it. Her use of process theology is useful, because the basic assumption of truth as every evolving, and in need of re-examination in various contexts, reflects the ever-changing urban context.[63] The practices of analysis and reflection brought to concrete and very real contextual challenges make process theology a useful partner in the work of urban multicultural ministry. She uses the case study method to engage the particularities of the lived experience of communities. To be presented with a detailed description of a context or situation, to question, analyze, and reflect on that particular experience, invites assessments and judgments that can then be brought to and tested in other contexts. For students it invites analysis with concrete truths, as opposed to theoretical possibilities.[64] Robert A. Evans and Thomas D. Park have edited a volume using this methodology in Christian theology[65] and Botkin, Elmandjra and Malitza[66] use it to plan education for the future. This methodology is also part of the pedagogical models of Robert and Alice Evans, William B. Kennedy, and Thomas Parker, and Thomas Groome's dialogical sharing also uses this methodology.[67] The engagement of process theology and the case study method of teaching enrich the description of each case, invite engagement with the context, and acknowledge the mystery or limits of knowledge present in any situation that is being studied and taught.[68] The open-endedness of the discussions produced, allows for flexibility of practice, a necessary skill for leaders in today's constantly changing contexts.

In engaging gestalt methodology, teaching becomes an integrative process that engages the insights of psychology, sociology, and anthropology.[69] Learning through problem solving, and through seeing discrete things as part of a whole, parts in

---

[62] Mary Elizabeth Moore, *Teaching from the Heart: Theology and Educational Method* (Harrisburg, Pennsylvania: Trinity Press International, 1980), 6.
[63] Moore, *Teaching from the Heart,* 18.
[64] Moore, *Teaching from the Heart,* 28.
[65] Moore, *Teaching from the Heart,* 30.
[66] Moore, *Teaching from the Heart,* 35.
[67] Moore, *Teaching from the Heart,* 31-51.
[68] Moore, *Teaching from the Heart,* 46-58.
[69] Moore, *Teaching from the Heart,* 59.

relation to each other, makes this a useful methodology for urban contexts, where people are engaged in situations that have many moving parts forming and influencing the whole.[70] We see a formational program that engages these gestalt principles in Westerhoff's use of the liturgical year as an organizing principle for the many disparate parts of a faith community's life and educational programs.[71] For communities whose identity and history is often negated because their minority status in a dominant culture that emphasizes linear time and progress, the engagement of process theology with this educational methodology theoretically takes seriously their past, their culture, and their experiences. Thus as issues are resolved and re-emerge, they are not responded to as irrelevant but as an important component in the problem solving and learning in which the community is engaged.[72] From these various confluences new things, new solutions, new possibilities emerge, the process concept of novelty is operative. "The idea of novelty explains how new forms of unity can emerge, both from new patterns of organizing the past and from new influences."[73] Such a pedagogy engages leaders to see the patterns, ask open-ended questions, and to take seriously how structure is impacting the context, providing more possibilities to engage the problem with solutions that are outside the box but that take seriously what is in the background, what is brought to the present from the past.[74]

Phenomenological methodology, or incarnational teaching, invites openness to the engagement with the other, teacher and student, student and student, or present learners/thinkers with past learners/thinkers.[75] This intersubjectivity respects the possibilities and the limitations inherent in our subjectivity. It also respects the interdependence inherent in life and by extension in meaning. Hence, "we can expect that what is revealed in the life of one person or community will be related and significant to the life of others."[76] The task and process of listening and learning from each other's stories and experiences, the ways each makes sense of the world and

---

[70] Moore, *Teaching from the Heart*, 61.
[71] Moore, *Teaching from the Heart*, 82.
[72] Moore, *Teaching from the Heart*, 74.
[73] Moore, *Teaching from the Heart*, 76.
[74] Moore, *Teaching from the Heart*, 89.
[75] Moore, *Teaching from the Heart*, 92.
[76] Moore, *Teaching from the Heart*, 93.

the knowledge each brings, allows knowledge, truth, and understanding to come forth through the engagement.[77] The respectful openness to each person's experience, without seeking to make it fit a model or system of thought, allows for engagement and learning that can often be limited because of strategies that necessarily cannot contain the whole of the experience/reality.[78] Ross and Martha Snyder's work in religious education utilizes phenomenology, a methodology that allows the listener to learn from the description of the experience on its own terms.[79]

The relational narrative teaching method capitalizes on the sharing of stories,[80] Moore argues for the use of narrative as a methodology in itself, rather than as a method or tool to be used in a goal or process.[81] Aspects of this can be seen in Harris's discussion of the role of imagination in education, and in Robert Coles work on listening and telling stories, if one extends it into the work of education and moral development.[82] Engaging stories, as we do in the biblical and religious traditions, involves more of the person in the process of learning, and encourages the use of the imagination in the process of social critique and cultural transmission.[83] She neatly summarizes the importance of engaging each other's narratives for the work of multicultural urban ministry:

> We need this variety to help people cross over into other forms of consciousness and to see the world from the perspectives of others. This is important to living in a pluralistic world and to the self-development that we call education.[84]

Moore ends with a discussion of the liberative or conscientizing method of teaching, affirming that both theology and education are, or should be, liberative tasks.[85] Engaging and dismantling oppressive and destructive systems is part of the life affirming work of theology and education. Paolo Freire's conscientizing method

---

[77] Moore, *Teaching from the Heart*, 102.
[78] Moore, *Teaching from the Heart*, 114.
[79] Moore, *Teaching from the Heart*, 99.
[80] Moore, *Teaching from the Heart*, 131.
[81] Moore, *Teaching from the Heart*, 136.
[82] Moore, *Teaching from the Heart*, 138-9.
[83] Moore, *Teaching from the Heart*, 139.
[84] Moore, *Teaching from the Heart*, 158.
[85] Moore, *Teaching from the Heart*, 163.

invited people to "name oppressions and re-form social reality."[86] This methodology as presented by Freire (and to be discussed later in this chapter), assumes that education is not neutral; it either serves to transform oppressive structures or it supports the oppressive status quo.[87] Moore cites the work of Groome, Harris, and Schipani as examples of liberative pedagogy in religious education. Groome identifies five movements in this action-reflection process: description of one's own or society's praxis, identifying stories and visions that underlie that praxis, reflection on the Christian story and vision, dialogical reflection between one's own (or society's) praxis and vision and that of the Christian story, and finally decisions (and actions) for a renewed praxis.[88] Maria Harris's liberative pedagogy draws from feminist theory and focuses on the teacher and the teaching act as central to the liberative process. Using dancing as a metaphor, steps that lead to one another but are not linear, she identifies the step of "silence, political awareness, mourning, bonding, and birthing," and thus broadens action-reflection to incorporate the process of listening, grieving, and celebrating that are part of the transformation process.[89] This addition is especially applicable in congregations in the urban setting where traditions, practices and cultures that were dominant in the past are lost, or must be diminished to allow for what is new and changing in the context and community where ministry is happening today. Specifically, the reality of grief and the need to lament are necessary in order for transformation to move into celebration. For Schipani, the liberating process of engaging and appropriating the gospel in one's own life is brought into focus, and the reflection on that narrative is empowering.[90] This shares elements of other occasions where listening and narrative are identified as important. Thus, the centrality of the sharing of the liberative Gospel as the task of Christian Education nuances the role of the scriptural narrative. Liberative pedagogies, and even liberation theologies, are enhanced by process theology's understanding of God as needing to collaborate with humanity in order to bring liberation and freedom to all of creation. "God does

---

[86] Moore, *Teaching from the Heart,* 164.
[87] Moore, *Teaching from the Heart,* 169.
[88] Moore, *Teaching from the Heart,* 172.
[89] Moore, *Teaching from the Heart,* 173.
[90] Moore, *Teaching from the Heart,* 174.

not have all of the power in the world…the very existence of human freedom suggests that human beings themselves have some power, and they can use that power for liberation or for destruction."[91] Process theology in turn is grounded in the social analysis required by liberative methodologies, fleshing out the contextual in reflection and analysis of the systems that oppress and the lived experience of the oppressed.[92] This dialogue between these different pedagogies and process theology provides a wide range of methodologies that can inform the task of leadership development in urban, multicultural contexts. They share a common vision, namely that the purpose of religious education and formation is to free the human person to be fully alive in the presence of God, and actively engaged in God's will, but these Christian values are grounded in history, and are responsive to the ever-present task of resisting and transforming oppressive realities. Social justice education, as these scholars argue, is a central part of Christian formation. Religious education, its interdisciplinary approach and emphasis on social transformation, are not novel innovations to Christian formation; they are at the heart of the task and have been present from the inception of the field.

Social Justice Religious Education

This project of religious education has also been a multidisciplinary project from its formal inception. George Albert Coe, who because of his involvement with the Religious Education Association from its beginning and throughout his lifetime is known as the father of religious education, integrated the social sciences, the scientific method and social analysis in his understanding of the task of religious education. He brought a critical lens to his social analysis, in this parting with the progressive education movement, to identify the oppressiveness of the social systems.[93] His understanding of religious education as a process of critical thinking about issues of faith, God, and church, and his recognition that these subjects should be investigated using scientific methods, also

---

[91] Moore, *Teaching from the Heart*, 177.
[92] Moore, *Teaching from the Heart*, 190-4.
[93] Helen Allan Archibald, "George A. Coe," Talbot School of Theology: Protestant Educators,
accessed September 29, 2014,
http://www.talbot.edu/ce20/educators/protestant/george_coe/.

challenges religious educators to see social change, and social justice as central to their work.[94] The basic methodology of social analysis, critical engagement, and the importance of church and believers' action to seek social justice provide a foundation for the kind of formation that lay leaders engage in multicultural urban ministry need today. These themes are treated both in social justice religious education and in secular critical multicultural education.

The centrality of Catholic Social Teaching in the Roman Catholic tradition has meant multiple resources for social justice religious education. The topics are not inclusive of all issues that many consider central in social justice education, but the use of the see-judge-act methodology, and the contributions to issues of class and the environment have been utilized beyond the Roman Catholic Church. *Living Justice and Peace: Catholic Social Teaching in Practice* is a textbook that provides an overview to the church history, theology, ethics and practice that is grounded in Catholic Social Teaching.[95] This book presents the Pastoral Circle, or Circle of Praxis, as a way to put faith into action.[96] Thomas Massaro prepared a similar resource, geared towards a different audience. *Living Justice: Catholic Social Teaching in Action* presents the social ethics of the Roman Catholic Church in an accessible way for seekers and novices, along with reflection questions.[97] Each of these resources seeks to engage the student in reflections on faith that will lead to action in the world that reflect the moral, ethical teaching of the faith tradition. Each offers an understanding of discipleship, witnessing to the faith held, as central to faithful, lived practice. Two examples of protestant resources for social justice religious education are *Pedagogies for the Non-Poor* and *Pedagogy of the Poor: Building the Movement to End Poverty*.[98] Alice Frazier Evans, Robert A. Evans and

---

[94] George A. Coe, *A Social Theory of Religious Education* (New York: Charles Scribner's Sons, 1917) Coe's seminal work that brings together these various fields in service of religious education.

[95] Jerry Windley-Daoust, *Living Justice and Peace: Catholic Social Teaching in Practice* (Winona, Minnesota: Saint Mary's Press, 2008).

[96] Windley-Daoust, *Living Justice and Peace*, 78.

[97] Thomas Massaro, S.J., *Living Justice, Catholic Social Teaching in Action* (New York: Rowan & Littlefield, 2011), ix.

[98] Alice Frazier Evans, Robert A. Evans and William Bean Kennedy, *Pedagogies for the Non-Poor* (Chicago: University of Chicago Press, 1988), and Willie Baptist and

William Bean Kennedy offer a theoretical and theological framework for congregations engaging in social justice practices in their local contexts. They present case studies, of congregations and church organizations engaging in these ministries. They review the strategies and leadership models employed as examples of how each church analyzed its context, reflected on its traditions and experience, planned and executed action, and then reflected on that action and decided upon next steps. Especially helpful in each case study is the presentation of the challenges, resistance, accommodation, and changes that were required as these congregations engaged in ministry. The local initiatives and the lay and clergy involvement in the development and implementation of these projects, make the case studies a useful resource for congregations seeking to respond to the oppressive forces that impact their local communities.

In *Pedagogy of the Poor,* Willie Baptist and Jan Rehmann present case studies of community engagement in response to issues of poverty. They use an interdisciplinary approach to analyze the issues that create poverty, and present a model of collaboration between those who are interested in ministry and those who are working for social change from a secular perspective. The resource seeks to equip and support the action-reflection model in which they are engaged to affect change. In many contexts there are people working for social change that are not involved in congregational life and there are people of faith interested in social change that have not had real life experience with community leaders engaged in this work. The text provides theological, philosophical, and academic resources for the work of reflection on activism, and strategies for community members to share the lessons of their experience and first-hand knowledge of structures and systems of oppression that reinforce poverty conditions. This dialogue and cross-fertilization creates a rich resource for use in leadership development. The resource is grounded in the work of diverse people engaging urban contexts.

These resources provide specific strategies for organizing and equipping congregations to engage in social justice ministries. Other resources focus on the living out of the commitment to social justice

---

Jan Rehmann, *Pedagogy of the Poor: Building the Movement to End Poverty* (New York: Teachers College Press, 2011).

ministry principles, not in the wider community, but within the workings of the church community itself. One such resource is Joseph Barndt's *Becoming an Anti-Racist Church: Journeying toward Wholeness*.[99] Recognizing that most churches in the United States continue to reflect in their racial composition the legacy of racism, Barndt seeks to guide congregations interested in changing this reality through a process that will assist them in living into their anti-racist values. The sections teach about the impact of historical racism on churches, and provide examples that show how structures and practices keep this reality alive in churches today. It also provides questions for individuals and groups to reflect on their own experiences and knowledge in order to act in a way that dismantles racism within the church. Of particular interest to this text's topic is the discussion on multiculturalism and racism within the church.[100] The definitions of culture, race-based culture, cultural racism, white cultural identity, and multicultural diversity clarify terms that, because they are often used interchangeably, make discussions of power and privilege difficult and confusing. Its discussion within the context of becoming an anti-racist church provides a corrective to some discussions of multiculturalism that seek to circumvent uncritically the issues of power and oppression that are present in diverse congregations. An honest discussion of issues of power and domination in the church allows obstacles that arise when seeking to increase diversity in all facets of congregational life to be addressed.[101] This invites institutional changes that support the efforts of anti-racism and multiculturalism/diversity processes instead of hindering them. The work is rightly framed as long term, and the various stages are presented as a continuum on which many churches can identify their progress towards becoming and sustaining an anti-racist church.

Stephanie Spellers offers a similar resource with her *Radical Welcome: Embracing God, the Other, and the Spirit of Transformation*.[102] Through case studies of congregations that have adopted principles and practices of inclusion, Spellers invites readers to engage

---

[99] Joseph Barndt, *Becoming an Anti-Racist Church: Journeying Toward Wholeness* (Minneapolis: Fortress, 2011).
[100] Barndt, *Becoming an Anti-Racist Church,* 133-44.
[101] Barndt, *Becoming an Anti-Racist Church,* 143-4.
[102] Spellers, *Radical Welcome.*

reflection questions that help them assess their congregation's own practices of inclusion, and to identify the next steps, both personal and structural, through which the congregation will become more welcoming of the stranger. Her definition of the ministry of radical inclusion also addresses directly the issues of power and domination that are involved in multicultural ministry. "Radical welcome is a fundamental spiritual practice, one that combines the universal Christian ministry of welcome and hospitality with a clear awareness of power and patterns of inclusion and exclusion."[103] This resource provides both content for learning about issues confronting churches seeking to do this ministry of social justice in their context and a process for engaging the material in dialogue with the lived experience of the students, so as to act in a way that transforms the current unjust practices. Action-reflection is the methodology of these resources for congregations seeking internal transformation in order to engage the wider community and its issues, having practiced what they preach in their own communal life.

These two mainline denominational resources (Lutheran and Episcopal respectively) are written for a broader audience. Their contexts and perspectives, however, are especially appropriate for use in mainline liberal congregations, although they also offer resources appropriate for other contexts.

Mark Lau Branson and Juan F. Martinez present a similar project with referents that make it appropriate for more evangelical and conservative congregations. *Churches, Cultures and Leadership: A Practical Theology of Congregations and Ethnicities*[104] seeks to equip congregational leaders interested in participating in a ministry that engages people of different cultures, races, and economic circumstances. They offer an in-depth study of culture and cultural influences, and engage the reader in reflection questions that prompt them to become aware of their own culture and its impact on their understanding of their society, their church, and their own engagement in structures that work against reconciliation. Both in terms of audience and analysis, the book does not focus on issues of domination and power, instead couching the process as a response

---

[103] Spellers, *Radical Welcome*, 11.
[104] Mark Lau Branson and Juan F. Martinez, *Churches, Cultures and Leadership: A Practical Theology of Congregations and Ethnicities* (Madison, Wisconsin: InterVarsity Press, 2011).

to the changing contexts, increased social pluralism, and intercultural engagement that need to be intentionally engaged. The call is to reconciliation, a call from a God seeking reconciliation and salvation for all of creation. The authors present reflection and action as five interactive practical theology steps that facilitate this intentional engagement.[105] The book offers a great deal of information about culture, language, and social, cross-cultural engagement. The book is the product of classes taught in seminary and other ministry contexts for leaders preparing for ministry in a world in which past assumptions about the monocultural nature of church can no longer be sustained if the church is to stay relevant. It argues well the importance of an interdisciplinary approach, one that is engaged with the social sciences, by invoking the authority of scripture, read through an intercultural lens.

The second edition provides additional Bible study resources for congregational leaders to ground and provide a framework for their reflections on culture and society, and the implications of these shifts for the ministry of the church in times of great change and pluralism. The second edition also includes an acknowledgement of the pernicious issues of race present in church and society. Written in 2023, in a sociopolitical climate of increased awareness of racial violence and discrimination as well as counter movements for racial justice, the revision emphasizes "the profound continuing power of racism, including how churches are too frequently participants in the societal wounds and inequities."[106] The discussion of social constructs in chapter 3, "Sociocultural Structures, Ethnicity, and Churches," is made more descriptive of the U.S. context through the inclusion of issues of race. The editing of the chapter to engage race more fully is seen in the section on "Colonization, Caste, and Race."[107] The authors reflect on the influence of scholars of racism on their thinking and the importance of including, even highlighting it in a text that is primarily reflecting on congregational life through the lens of ethnicity. Their critical engagement of issues of systemic racism introduces the reality of power in society and in church systems. As such this text is an excellent model of leadership formation in congregations seeking to become ethnically diverse. Its

---

[105] Branson and Martinez, *Churches, Cultures and Leadership,* 42-50.

[106] Branson and Martinez, *Churches, Cultures and Leadership,* second edition, 22, (Downers Grove, IL: InterVarsity Press, 2023)

[107] Branson and Martinez, *Churches, Cultures and Leadership,* second edition, 88-94.

practical theology methodology reflects critical multicultural education pedagogical practice. And although focused on ethnicity, it offers strategies for congregations to study and learn about differences that can be adapted for use with communities interested in inclusion of people of other varied identity differences.

Sheryl Kujawa-Holbrook offers a resource that provides in-depth case studies that model how anti-racist commitments can be lived out in community. Her text, *A House of Prayer for All Peoples: Congregations Building Multiracial Community*, describes the process undertaken by congregations that are committed to becoming congregations that reflect the racial justice they believe they are called to embody as people of faith.[108] The introduction provides excellent definitions of terms that are often misused or misunderstood, and of the values and characteristics that reflect an attention to power, structures and practices of domination that define racist structures.[109] Though not organized as a resource for study, it nonetheless teaches readers through the case studies to reflect on the various strategies that different congregations adopt in different contexts. As Moore notes, case studies allow those studying them to see a concrete example of different ways to address similar challenges of racism and oppression. It is inspiring to see what is being done in various communities, especially about an issue that seems so intractable.

The last text I would like to review is *Multicultural Religious Education* edited by Barbara Wilkerson.[110] This collection of essays addresses issues of race and ethnicity, and because they cut across all the groups discussed, there is some discussion of issues of class and gender.[111] However, the book includes no discussion of issues of disability and access or of sexuality. The latter might be explained by the stance taken in the text, one that seeks to be politically neutral and to avoid a "relativistic approach to religion."[112] The book seeks to address the reality of diversity and pluralism, without directly tackling issues of power and oppression that impact the disenfranchised in urban contexts. It seeks to re-engage church

---

[108] Sheryl A. Kujawa-Holbrook, *A House of Prayer for All Peoples: Congregations Building Multiracial Community* (Bethesda, Maryland: The Alban Institute, 2002).
[109] Kujawa-Holbrook, *A House of Prayer for All Peoples*, 1-25.
[110] Wilkerson, *Multicultural Religious Education*.
[111] Wilkerson, *Multicultural Religious Education*, 3.
[112] Wilkerson, *Multicultural Religious Education*, 3-4.

leaders who may have dismissed multicultural education because of the controversies that this topic has engendered in the public sphere.[113] The desire to avoid conflict and controversy often determined which theologies these church leaders engaged as dialogue partners; they often selected only those that provide a "basis for unity and tolerance in multicultural dialogue."[114]

Multicultural Religious Education has adopted some of the empowerment and justice values in its goals, such as a curriculum that reflects diversity, a participatory model of leadership that promotes leadership, emphasis on communication and dialogue and action employed to be socially responsible for reducing inequalities.[115] The essays then provide theological, philosophical, and pedagogical foundations for multicultural religious education. The contributors to the volume each utilize an interdisciplinary approach to the various topics: scripture, pedagogical approaches, and structural and institutional change. The topics provide a foundation for those interested in multicultural religious education in a variety of contexts, but do not directly provide tools and strategies for equipping lay leaders in urban contexts to develop and sustain inclusive congregations that seek justice and social transformation.

Conclusion

The literature on urban church ministry confirms the need for having trained lay ministers who can successfully minister to the city, and the scarcity of resources to do so. The literature on social justice ministry provides strategies and tools for engaging in social justice ministry in urban (and other) contexts. These texts utilize case studies and interdisciplinary analysis and frameworks for studying urban ministry and justice ministries. Some of these texts focus on issues of poverty, race, and intercultural relations. None engages directly the intersectionality of these and other issues of oppression as they impact urban congregations. The need to consider together the various strands of oppression in order to provide a multifaceted, complex approach to leadership development can be addressed by engaging the strategies and

---

[113] Wilkerson, *Multicultural Religious Education,* 2.
[114] Wilkerson, *Multicultural Religious Education,* 5.
[115] Wilkerson, *Multicultural Religious Education,* 27.

methods of critical multicultural education. Both the process and the goals seek to create leaders equipped to address and respond to the forces that are impacting urban communities and their churches, in order to transform them to reflect more fully the gospel values of justice.

CHAPTER THREE

Saint Mary's Episcopal Church, Los Angeles

Case Study

Case Study of Urban Multicultural Congregation #1: The multicultural nature of this Japanese American congregation, and its ever-expanding diversity, have created leaders that know how to survive oppression in the long haul, but have not been equipped to change the structures of oppression.

As of 2014, the annual celebration of the Christmas Festival has changed a great deal over the years at St. Mary's Episcopal Church, in Koreatown, Los Angeles.[1] The Sunday school, a keystone of the congregation for the first seventy-five years of its existence, was key in celebrating this annual tradition. The ever-diminishing attendance at Sunday school has made the planning of the event a greater challenge than usual in recent years. Many St. Mary's families live in the suburbs, and regular Sunday School attendance has been low for many years. The parish profiles for the last two rector searches have presented this low attendance as an ongoing concern, and have sought a rector who could help the church get families with children to join the parish again, making it a priority for the parish leadership. Most of those who express such hopes dream in particular of Japanese American families becoming active and populating the Sunday School in the way it once was. The identity of this parish as a center of Japanese American life in Los Angeles remains strong; it is a heritage of which parishioners are proud and which they wish to continue. And to their credit they

---

[1] Sunday, December 21st, 2014, Christmas Festival, Bi-lingual and Multicultural combined services of St. Mary's Episcopal Church and Trinity Episcopal Church, both in Los Angeles, CA.

have explored what it's going to take for the dream to become reality and have accepted the need to become open to change and engagement in their diverse urban context so that they can be a vital parish again.[2]

Consequently, the church, with the leadership of the new rector, has reached out to the community with renewed vigor, building relationships with neighbors, collaborating on those projects that respond to their needs, dreams, and aspirations. Community cultural celebrations, such as involving neighbors who use the community gardens on to the grounds of the church, working with leaders of the Oaxacan community, seeking a place for their music programs and prayer practices, the collaborative ministry with another nearby Episcopal parish worshipping in English and Spanish — all these have led to a broader, larger community coming together for this annual Christmas celebration. This diversity is reflected in the celebration: children that reflect the heritage of the people of the community — Latin@, European-American, Japanese-American, and Oaxacan (Indigenous) — become the narrators of the Christmas story, dancers in the traditional Japanese dance group, the Kotobuki Kai liturgical dancers, and the Banda, playing tradition Oaxacan songs. A young Japanese American soloist performed a contemporary Christmas song and the Recorder beginners' class represented the spectrum of talent. Adults from Mexico, Guatemala, El Salvador, and Panama danced and sang. An older and a younger Japanese American member, leaders who have seen the church through many transitions, continued the long tradition of presenting staff and parish leaders with Christmas gifts. The celebration was busy, crowded, raucous, and full of vitality.

The journey to that celebration is one that is being lived by many urban mainline congregations. Yet the particular cultural heritage and history of this parish makes its case both distinctive and instructive for churches seeking to be responsive to a context with shifting demographics. It is especially instructive as a congregation that has endured injustices that are now being lived by its neighbors, injustices of racial, ethnic, and economic discrimination and disenfranchisement.

---

[2] Parish Profiles for both 2001 and 2010 identify ministry with children and youth and growing the Sunday School as priorities for their new rector. "St. Mary's Parish Profile, 2010," St. Mary's Parish, Los Angeles, accessed October 2, 2014, http://stmarys-la.org/lang/en/history/parish-profile/.

The congregation of St. Mary's Episcopal Church was founded to serve and care for a community of immigrants that was under siege in the Los Angeles area in 1907.[3] Mary Louise Paterson began the mission, having spent time as a missionary in Japan. Her adopted daughter, Mary Tsune Tanaka, married (Father) John Misao Yamazaki, who became the mission pastor, then the first vicar of St. Mary's Church. Paterson's inspiration to mission work came from a performance of the *Magnificat* (hence the parish's name) that reflected on the impact that Mary and her story of service had on Paterson's life. St. Mary's was located at the heart of the Japanese immigrant community, and assisted immigrants with assimilation into the new culture. Services were offered in English and Japanese to accommodate the Issei (immigrant) and Nissei (first generation) members of the community.[4] These Christian families sought to become American, working and contributing to their new home and establishing their families in hopes of benefiting from the American Dream. The tight-knit community provided a network that eased the adjustment. But it also fueled the suspicion, mistrust, and bigotry of the dominant culture surrounding them. In 1941 the church building on Mariposa Street replaced the house church on Flower Street amid signs that warned "Japs Keep Moving: This is a White Man's Neighborhood" during the Depression. On Sunday morning signs warning about the reduction of property values if the church were allowed to build a parish hall had to be removed before services. There was no subtlety to the message that these Japanese immigrants were not welcome.[5]

The legacy of race and racism in U.S. society affected immigration and citizenship policy and practice, and that included

---

[3] A comprehensive and detailed history of the church's first 100 years can be found in the "St. Mary's Episcopal Church 1907-2007, Centennial Booklet, 2007" and has served to provide the material for this case study along with the "St. Mary's Parish, 2001" and "St. Mary's Parish Profile, 2010," prepared for the rector searches being conducted at that time.
[4] Later on, Japanese immigrants from Hawaii would also be integrated into the church, their experience of immigration, decidedly different, weaving into the other differences that would create a multicultural fabric.
[5] Joanna B. Gillespie, "Japanese-American Episcopalians During World War II: The Congregation of St. Mary's Los Angeles, 1941-1945," Uncovered Voices, Women's 'Pious Memoirs' and Other Mostly Ignored Voices from the Episcopal Church in the 18th and 19th cc, last modified 2009, http://www.joannabgillespie.com/articleinteredjapanese.html.

the place of Japanese immigrants.[6] The nation that was established on the ideal of the equality of all men reserved the right to define humanity along lines of racial distinction. This racial discrimination became codified in the laws and ordinances that defined citizenship in the U.S. based on whiteness and limited the full participation of others who were defined as non-white in society. The Constitution with its rights and protections in practice did not include all who lived and worked to build the nation. Early scientific methodology was applied to the task of understanding the differences in the races, presumed to be inherent, which explained the reality of white dominance and Black subjugation.[7] Scientists studied and established a hierarchy of racial superiority, with whites at the top, and defined others as less than them, inferior, and therefore disqualified from full participation as citizens of the republic. Citizenship was conferred on those identified as white as defined by Aryan ancestry and cranial measurements. This negatively impacted Japanese immigrants and their Japanese-American children striving to integrate into American society. Only those designated as white were accorded the right to become citizens and to benefit from the privileges of citizenship.

Several cases challenging this definition of "American" arose, culminating in the case of Takao Ozawa vs. the United States.[8] Ozawa argued that having lived in the U.S. for twenty years, having attended U.S. high schools and colleges, spoken English in his home, raised his children as Americans, and as being a moral, productive member of American society, he qualified as a U.S. citizen. The decision rendered by the Supreme Court stated that because he was

---

[6] For a discussion of the immigration policies based on race, and specifically definitions of whiteness as it impacted Japanese immigrants see, Mae M. Ngai, "The Architecture of Race in American Immigration Law: A Reexamination of the Immigration of Act of 1924," *The Journal of American History* 86, no. 1 (June 1999): 67-92.

[7] For a review of the history of the use of scientific methodologies to create the category of whiteness and affirm its superiority in the subjugation of the Black race see Desmond King, *Making Americans: Immigration, Race, and the Origins of Diverse Democracy* (Cambridge: Harvard University Press, 2000).

[8] A summary of the law, "U.S. Supreme Court Takao Ozawa v. US, 260 U.S. 178 (1922)" can be found on the website, Find Law, for Legal Professionals, accessed January 8, 2015, http://caselaw.lp.findlaw.com/cgi-bin/getcase.pl?court=US&vol=260&invol=178. A discussion of the immigration laws' construction of racial categories is found in Ngai, "The Architecture of Race," 81-86.

born in Japan and was not white, he could not be an American citizen; naturalization at that time was restricted to free whites and persons from Africa and of African descent. By extension, if Japanese persons could not be citizens they could not own property, which led to the confiscation of property and lands. This fueled and further supported the racist attitudes held by whites in the U.S. towards Japanese Americans, and other immigrants. The argument, based on "scientific" findings, that whites were Caucasians and descendants of Aryan lineage, and that Japanese persons did not share this heritage did nothing to help the appeal for citizenship of Indian immigrants who did share this heritage. In United States vs. Bhagat Singh Thind,[9] the scientific methodology that traced Caucasian lineage to Aryan descendants was deemed problematic and no longer reliable as a measure of whiteness. Instead of an argument based upon obscure scientific measures, the simple and clear definition of whiteness would be taken from the language of the citizenship qualification itself, that of "free white men." This definition was obvious to the common man, and was the intention of the lawmakers, and would further define whiteness as a characteristic of European Americans, regardless of their country of origin. Not only did this define Indians as not eligible for citizenship, but persons who had been naturalized prior to this decision were stripped of their citizenship, and by extension their properties, and their rights.

The racism against Asians, the contempt and distrust of people of "oriental" descent, and the role of these in European imperialism has been well documented in Edward Said's seminal work, *Orientalism*.[10] The worldview and attitude he describes was operative in treatment of Asians in the United States, especially in the Los Angeles area. Those running for public office appealed to this populist view, and political posters and placards of the period

---

[9] A summary of the law, "U.S. Supreme Court U.S. v. Bhagat Singh Thind, 261 U.S. 204 (1923)" can be found on the website, Find Law for Legal Professionals, accessed January 8, 2015, http://caselaw.lp.findlaw.com/scripts/getcase.pl?navby=CASE&court=US&vol =261&page=204. A discussion of the law's role in the construction of whiteness by exclusion of people of Asian descent is in Ngai, "The Architecture of Race," 81-86.
[10] Edward W. Said, *Orientalism* (New York: Random House, 1979).

blatantly expressed it.[11] Their "difference," their "exoticness" made such persons impossible to integrate, they alleged, a difference described and defined by their cultural and religious practices, dress, and features. This understanding was reflected even in church journals as seen in an article in *The Living Church*.[12]

For the members of the congregation of St. Mary's the dominant culture's rejection served only to further motivate them to show their loyalty and worthiness by more perfectly assimilating the dominant groups' culture, values, traditions, practices, and lifestyles. They were good Christians, who wore western dress, learned English, and learned and engaged in the lifestyles and pastimes of other Americans. When Pearl Harbor was bombed, the congregation was gathered for worship. The community was as shocked, outraged and saddened as other Americans at this unprovoked attack.[13]

In the face of the increasing discrimination and bigotry that followed Pearl Harbor, the members of St. Mary's continued, under the leadership of their pastor to be stoically compliant and steadfast in their loyalty to their new home country. When executive order 9066 led to the internment of Japanese Americans, the community of St. Mary's went quietly to the detention centers. John Yamazaki, Jr., the senior pastor's son, was ordained and married, and prepared as assistant pastor to the congregation, to accompany and care for his people in the internment camps. Society's arguments that supported this detention ranged from the need to protect the Japanese people from the anger and fear of the general population to the need to sequester this community that was a threat to the "American" way of life.[14] St. Mary's Church served as a gathering and departure point for the camps. Seven hundred people in cars, trucks, and buses were transported from St. Mary's on Easter

---

[11] LA City Council Candidates argued that it was the fault of Japanese immigrants that property values and economic opportunities of good Americans had been negatively impacted. One of these political posters is featured in a history board that St. Mary's Episcopal Church prepared to present the history of the church.
[12] Ngai uses the term "unassimilable" to describe the assumption that people, defined as racially Asiatic, could not blend into the American landscape, which was systematically being defined exclusively as White American. See also Gillespie, "Japanese-American Episcopalians," 2-3.
[13] Gillespie, "Japanese-American Episcopalians," 2.
[14] Gillespie, "Japanese-American Episcopalians," 9.

Monday, April 1942.[15] Family property and possessions were sold at a great loss, given away, or abandoned. Some African American neighbors stored things for families, supporting their friends in hopes of a time when they could rebuild their lives. The Episcopal Church also bought some of the properties to preserve them for the detainees to reclaim after the internment period. But this was not true of every property. This meant that devalued property was promptly bought, and the demographics and the nature of the neighborhood changed dramatically overnight.[16] The people of St. Mary's accepted this internment as a part of being a good American citizen.

The Episcopal Church made other efforts to make the experience less difficult. For example, they requested that the community be interned together. Despite the Church's efforts, the congregation was divided among different camps with most residing in Gila Bend, Arizona and Jerome, Arkansas. The priests were able to go with their flock and to provide pastoral care while in interment.[17] The Episcopal Church was able to assure that they would be allowed to conduct their own worship, instead of participating in the general protestant worship. Through continued contact with Episcopal organizations and leadership they were encouraged to be steadfast, and were provided the materials necessary to create worship spaces that allowed them to continue practicing within their tradition uninterrupted. Although many were outraged at the passage of this executive order and the ill treatment that was endured by this community, the Church's dominant strategy seemed to be to wait for the end of this terrible time, and in the meanwhile to encourage and support the Episcopalians in the camps as they survived this injustice. At the 1943 Convention of the Episcopal Diocese of Los Angeles, Bishop Stevens spoke about the unjust discrimination and racism being endured by minorities, in an effort to educate delegates about the appropriate Christian response, and to remind them that these too were members of the body of Christ.[18] The loyalty of the priests in internment to their church and nation not only meant compliance but also that they would act as faithful citizens in cooperating with the government.

---

15 Gillespie, "Japanese-American Episcopalians," 5.
16 Gillespie, "Japanese-American Episcopalians," 5.
17 Gillespie, "Japanese-American Episcopalians," 6-7.
18 Gillespie, "Japanese-American Episcopalians," 8.

Other Japanese who were interned, who regarded this injustice, as something to be resisted not accepted, saw this loyalty as collaboration. Father John Yamazaki, Sr. suffered at their hands; they felt that his compliance and cooperation with the government was perpetuating the injustice toward them and amounted to collaboration with the enemy. After he assisted in the enlistment for the all-Japanese troops to fight in the war, Father John was beaten so badly he had to be taken to the infirmary. He reflected on the experience later as part of the sacrifice he had made for people as their pastor, never questioning his duty as a Christian to include cooperation with his (American) government. Americanism and Christianity were synonymous to him. Faithfulness to the denomination and to the nation was definitive of their shared identity and culture as immigrants. They sought to be loyal Americans, to accept the laws and judgment of the nation's leadership.

In 1943 the interment order was lifted, and families began to leave the camps. Some returned to the neighborhood they had left behind, but most did not. Many were homeless and St. Mary's Church became a place that housed and supported families as they transitioned from the camps. In this way the church continued its mission to support Japanese families in the process of acclimating to a new society, although this time the reintegration meant that many did not return to the old neighborhood.[19] Integration meant blending in, not standing out as a distinct immigrant community. The anti-Japanese sentiment had not disappeared overnight, and on fresh wounds, salty attitudes of discrimination persisted. The desire to be seen as American meant in part to participate in the growing suburban lifestyle as soldiers returned from the war and communities were built to accommodate the new families that needed housing. Many St. Mary's families moved to the suburbs and the nature of the church shifted from one that was serving its immediate community to one that served a commuter population. The loyalty of association, despite distance, with the congregation of St. Mary's continued for generations. Even today many who are not able to attend regularly because of age and distance continue to support their congregation as pledging members.

---

[19] "St. Mary's Parish Profile, 2001."

The Japanese American cultural identity of the community was significantly shaped by this World War II experience. The desire to integrate was sustained, as the internment was explained in part as the result of having been seen as other, because of the creation of a separate immigrant community. They were aliens, and could be distinguished as such. This now was to be avoided. Therefore, now to be Japanese American was to be more American than Americans themselves. They personified '50s suburban culture in their church activities, in their dress, their foods, etc., but also in the clubs and organizations of which they became part. The Boy Scouts, the Girls' Friendly Society, Golf Clubs, Crafts groups, and the popular St. Mary's Bazaar were the centers of activity and community. To be a faithful church member was to be involved in these activities, as they were an expression of service for the church and the wider community. St. Mary's Mission achieved parish status in 1956 with Father John H. M. Yamazaki, its second vicar, becoming its first rector. Organizations and clubs flourished. The identification of these organizations as the heart of parish life is reflected in the two most recent parish profiles where they continue to define not only the history, but also the overall character of the church. The membership of these groups has aged and dwindled, but they continue to organize the involvement of church members, and remain at the heart of the parish's identity. St. Mary's is a church in action, not in social justice demonstrations, or in charity to the indigent, but in social activities that maintained a strong network of fellowship and community among the membership, and which define their outreach to the broader community. In the '50s, members saw their activities and programs as a reflection of their commitment to their church, and they offered them as an opportunity for the community to come and know who they were and what they were about. St. Mary's was a wholesome American parish, as defined by the 1950s popular culture.

The community surrounding St. Mary's changed dramatically after that era. Other immigrants moved in and made it their home. Currently St. Mary's is in Koreatown, a neighborhood that is predominantly Latino and Korean. The population has grown, and it is a bustling urban area. According to statistics available in 2014, the immediate vicinity of St. Mary's has a population of 59,185, with the median age being 32.4 years. Seventy-eight percent are sixteen years of age and over (46,179). The diversity of the community is

45

mostly Latino, with 74.5 % being Latino (of any race) or 44,074 of the population. The 25.5% that do not identify as Hispanic/Latino, who identify as being of only one race, are: 31.9% white, 18.5% Asian, 3.7% Black or African American, and 1.1% American Indian and Alaska Natives. The majority of the Latinos are listed by category as Mexican at 36.5%. The twenty-seven percent of people that are Asian are 82% Korean, a not surprising percentage, given that St. Mary's is in the Koreatown area of Los Angeles. When the boundaries are drawn more naturally, by using the main streets that surround the church for about a mile around, the numbers shift.[20] Hispanic/Latino are 64% of the population with 49% being Mexican, the vast majority being Oaxacan. The Asian community is 27% of the whole, of whom 82% are Korean, 4% White, and 3% Black or African-American.

The population is almost evenly divided by gender with men comprising 51.1% and women 48.9% respectively. Families live in households (98.5%), the average being three person households. The majority of these households rent their housing unit, with 91% or 16,937 renting while only 9% of housing units are occupied by the owner (1,680). The majority of people living within the immediate vicinity of the church have achieved more than a high school education and some college, but few have bachelor's degrees. Approximately 31% have high school diplomas or an equivalent and 36.7% have some college or an associate's degree, while only 7% have a bachelor's degree or higher. Thirty-two percent of individuals live below the poverty level. Fifty-two percent of those under the poverty level are under the age of eighteen, and thirty percent are over the age of sixty-five. The majority of those under the poverty level are not people we would expect to be employed. Income levels categorized by educational levels show that the median earnings for persons with graduate or professional degrees is $42,292, with women earning $38,750 and men $46,902. It is a significant jump from those with bachelor's degrees, whose median income is $26,605.[21] The majority of residents in the community immediately surrounding St. Mary's (60%) earn $25,000 or less, while the median monthly rental price is $770. A person could

---

[20] These boundaries, which comprise approximately a 1-mile radius, are Western Avenue, Olympic Boulevard, Vermont Avenue, and Pico Boulevard.
[21] U.S. Census Bureau, "American Fact Finder," accessed December 1, 2014, http://factfinder.census.gov/faces/nav/jsf/pages/index.xhtml.

expect to spend almost $10,000 annually on rent alone, not accounting for utilities, food, and transportation, the most basic of living expenses.[22] For the community that lives within a one-mile radius of the church, the statistics of income show that 38% have an income less than $15,000 per year, with an additional 22% and 16% up to $24,999 and $34,999 respectively, making a total of 76% of people in the neighborhood living with an annual income of less than $35,000. The poverty statistics are more severe for families with children under the age of 18 and especially those with a female head of household; of these, **30.4% of families are below the poverty level with married couples comprising 22.2% and female householders 44.2%.**

Throughout the years, the parish has sought various ways to respond to the shift in demographics and needs in their local community. The church had many youth programs and activities. They ran their own preschool from 1967-1985, and a preschool continues to serve the community on the church property. There were summer programs and collaborations with the local YMCA, in addition to church groups and organizations. The parish thrived. The summer vacation program was an outreach program to the community that for twenty years provided safe and supervised activities for local children. In 2002, after some discussion and deliberation, the parish hired an associate to offer services in Spanish. Community programs geared toward the neighbors, among them guitar classes for youth, English as a Second Language classes, and exercise classes for adults, also served to reach out to neighbors. In 2006 the church broke ground on the Yamazki Memorial Community Garden, where local families and the Sunday school program plant and harvest fruits, vegetables, and flowers. This garden has been awarded grants from the City of Los Angeles, and is seen as a model of a collaborative project that improves the quality of life for the community. All of these activities and programs were consistent with the church's long history of community work, and the parish was designated a Jubilee Center in 2006 for its work engaging and serving the poor and oppressed. Yet

---

[22] Trulia, "Los Angeles Market Trends," accessed December 1, 2014, http://www.trulia.com/real_estate/los_angeles-california/market-trends/.

the integration of neighbors into the actual mainstream life of the congregation has been more challenging.

In their 2010 parish profile, the parish recognized that although their beloved Father John officially retired in 1985, his direct influence continued until his death in 1998, and that only recently, twenty-five years after his death has the parish been ready to shift the fundamental ways they operate in order to incorporate members of the neighborhood.[23] The legacy and continuity of the parish's leadership and vision can be seen in the calling of priests to serve in parish leadership. The clerical leadership of the parish was almost exclusively selected from within the church system. The parish search process, called leaders that provided continuity. The leadership that had been identified by the rector (or pastoral leader) succeeded that rector upon retirement or death. The missionary and church founder, Mary Louise Paterson, identified and worked with the Rev. John Misao Yamazaki, who became the first vicar of the parish. The Rev. Canon John H. M. Yamazaki, son of the vicar, became the assistant, and eventually the vicar and rector of the parish. The Rev. Mitsuo Paul Akiyoshi was called and served a relatively short term, 1986-1991, during which time there were conflicts over innovations in worship space, liturgy, and the calling of women to serve as assistants. At the end of his term the parish called the Rev. Kate Cullinane, who had been the assistant, to serve as the parish's third rector. The Rev. Alix Evans served first as part-time and then as full-time assistant, and upon Mother Kate's departure, became the fourth rector of the parish. The Rev. Marilyn Omernick, who had led a parish retreat, was asked by Mother Alix to cover her while she went on short-term disability. Sadly, Mother Alix died shortly after, and Mother Marilyn was appointed interim priest during the search that called the current rector. Each successive priest had already been trained and formed by working in the parish prior to taking on the role of Vicar/Rector. The congregation was familiar with each new priest before they were called, and the new priest was also familiar with how the systems operated within the parish. The continuity provided for a smooth transition from one leader to the next, on the one hand, and on the other hand did not provide the disruptions and learning that might come from adjusting to an unfamiliar leader, a new leadership style,

---

[23] "St. Mary's Church Parish Profile, 2010," 3.

and a review and restructuring of processes and systems. Instead, the church's hopes and dreams continued to be rooted in the church's past and in the achievements of a bygone time. The hope to have Japanese American families return to the church, to have many youth programs to serve these families and their children, and in this way to maintain the Japanese American identity of the parish remained central to the life and work of the church. The new material that is included in the parish profile reflects the conversations that were jumpstarted by the Rev. Richard Van Horn's sermon, and reflection work with the vestry on recovering the mission of the congregation. The parish profile reflects a process of reimagining the life of the church, and a commitment to accepting the changes necessary to respond to the shifts in their community and in the society as a whole.

The vestry minutes are informative in this respect. During Alix Evans' tenure as rector, around 2007-2008,[24] the parish participated in the Kaleidoscope Program offered by the Diocese to improve intercultural communications and engagements. But the program did not have much influence in what was decidedly a closed system. Leadership and decision making was still controlled by long-time leaders, who continued to run the parish and make decisions about programming in ways that were familiar and comfortable. Although not recorded specifically in the vestry minutes, there was some discussion of simply using the 2001 parish profile for the 2010 search process.[25]

The conversation about the future direction of the church was ongoing at the point of Mother Alix' death. Not only had the congregation's leaders participated in the Kaleidoscope training but also the theme of the parish retreat in 2008 was "Envisioning the Future of the Church (5-10 years)."[26] A walk around the neighborhood was to be part of the process of visioning during the retreat. The notes of the retreat only record that several issues about

---

[24] The material collected and used during the Kaleidoscope training by Eric H. F. Law in the Diocese of Los Angeles was purged as part of a parish clean-up project. The minutes available did not reference the training. The current rector confirms that it was early in Alix Evans tenure. Extensive training workshops in the Diocese of Los Angeles began in 2006.
[25] A conversation held with the current rector the Rev. Anna Olson, December 22, 2014.
[26] St. Mary's Episcopal Church, Vestry Minutes, May 11, 2008.

property repairs and management were discussed. Upon Mother Alix's death Mother Marilyn served as supply priest, and shortly thereafter was made interim priest in charge.[27] For the next year and a half the church prepared for the calling of a new rector. During that time there were many conversations about the future mission of the church while also embracing new collaborative opportunities for service. The Green RELAY program, a program the church had collaborated with before, sought support for a new program. It would give scholarships to a group of students to design and implement a service project that would facilitate social change in a significant way, specifically seeking to "amplify the impact of environmental justice groups in Los Angeles through movement building."[28] St. Mary's Church served as a site for housing the interns of the Episcopal Urban Intern Program of the Jubilee Consortium. In both of these collaborations St. Mary's rented out space for these programs to use, and supported the projects as community stakeholders.[29]

Each vestry meeting began with a time of reflection on materials on vestry and congregational development, continuing education for the leadership. The resources offered did not address the cultural issues present and impacting the visioning process for the vestry.[30] Although the cultural heritage and the shared experience of the

---

[27] The Rev. Alix Evans went on short-term disability leave on October 5, 2008, and The Rev. Marilyn Omernick served as supply. Mother Alix died on October 12, 2008, and Mother Marilyn was asked to serve half time as of October 13th, until an interim was identified. The minutes of December 14th record that the Priest in Charge letter of agreement was sent to the bishop for signature, and was offered for review to the vestry.

[28] St. Mary's Episcopal Church, Vestry Minutes, April 19, 2009.

[29] St. Mary's Episcopal Church, Vestry Minutes, March 21, 2010.

[30] Among the material distributed in the vestry meetings were Elizabeth Rankin Geitz's "Introduction" and "A Note for Vestry Members" in *Calling Clergy: A Spiritual and Practical Guide through the Search Process* (New York: Church Publishing, 2007), 1-4, 5-7, and Pierre Wolff, *Discernment: The Art of Choosing Well: Based on Ignatian Spirituality* (Ligouri, Missouri: Ligouri/Triumph, 2003); Arlin J. Rothauge, "Introduction," and "The Family Church: 0-50" in *Sizing Up a Congregation for New Member Ministry* (New York: The Episcopal Church Center, Seabury Professional Services, 1984), 1-2, 3-9, and Arlin J. Rothauge, "The Life Cycle Stages" and "Leadership in the Life Cycle Stages," in *The Life Cycle in Congregations: A Process of Natural Creation and An Opportunity for New Creation* (New York: Congregational Development Services, Episcopal Church Center, 1996), 3-8, 9-11.

congregation are central to the identity, hopes and fears of the congregation, the material did not facilitate a direct or open acknowledgement and discussion of these issues. The minutes do not record how the materials were used, or the nature of the conversations they initiated. There is, however, an indication that issues of communication were affecting the work of the leadership, vestry, and priest in charge for Eric Law's "Respectful Communication Guidelines"[31] was distributed, as was the article from the Alban Institute entitled, "Clean Up Bad Communication Habits,"[32] distributed in anticipation of a retreat that Bishop Diane Jardine Bruce was to lead with the congregation. The interim priest's contract, specifically the responsibility of the interim priest to "deal with internal conflicts and help heal divisions within the congregation,"[33] appears on vestry agendas multiple times. Each of these things suggests that communication issues were a concern. Communication is critical in any community situation, especially when the central task is reflection and discernment on the vision and future direction of the church. Yet in the material distributed to inform and facilitate the process, none were included that named the cultural differences that are reflected in communication styles.[34]

The assumption that open communication would mean direct communication without triangulation did not take into account that although St. Mary's members were very invested and proud of being Americans, the reality that they are Japanese Americans meant that communication respectful of relationships, and proper etiquette when addressing persons deserving respect because of their standing in the community (age for example) would be of high value. This would mean that indirect communication, or

---

[31] Eric H. F. Law, *The Bush was Blazing but Not Consumed: Developing a Multicultural Community through Dialogue and Liturgy* (St. Louis: Chalice, 1996).

[32] Alban, "Clean Up Bad Communication Habits," Alban at Duke Divinity School, May 19, 2008, accessed January 19, 2015, https://alban.org/archive/cleaning-up-bad-communication-habits/.

[33] For example, see St. Mary's Episcopal Church, Vestry Minutes, February 27, 2010.

[34] Eric H.F. Law in "A Dialogue Process: Focusing on Differences in Communication Styles," *The Bush Was Blazing But Not Consumed*, Appendix C, 154-7, discusses the differences in communication styles between high context and low context cultures. The exercises invite participants to identify their communication styles, can help leaders recognize the cultural differences at play in the communication styles of church members.

communication through an intermediary, or anonymously would be seen as appropriate, whereas direct communication would be seen as brash. Yet this cultural characteristic is defined as a "bad communication habit" to be avoided by churches at all costs.

There are also indications in the Minutes that communication difficulties and misgivings about change made it difficult to move on the intentions of collaborating and doing new things. One example was the distribution of an article that had appeared in the parish Young Adult ministry newsletter, The PEACE in 1992. In it, Glenn Kubota shares quotations from an article he discovered regarding the closing of a congregation in the diocese. The quotations reflect the missed opportunities for mission. The article spoke of the congregation's response (or lack of response) to the demographic shifts in the neighborhood that indicated it was in transition and the need for the church to plan appropriately to explore how to do mission in a new context. The St. Mary's newsletter article concludes with an example of an opportunity to do ministry with the Korean community in their neighborhood that was passed up by the vestry.[35] Another example of a missed opportunity for collaboration was the plan to develop with the Little Tokyo Service Center (LTSC) Transitional Housing for abused women. These plans were very far along in their development when it became clear that the necessary consensus was not present, and the plan was scrapped. Considering it is something that did not happen, it seems significant that it is listed in both the 2001 and the 2010 Parish Profiles. That this missed opportunity is memorialized reflects the church's lingering regrets regarding this project.[36]

The minutes reflect multiple discussions regarding mission, ministry, and visioning for the future. The materials already referenced, as well as others that discussed the various ways the church does ministry, the shared ministry of the laity and clergy and the role of the vestry and search committee were reviewed and discussed at vestry meetings.[37] The minutes reflect the sharing of

---

[35] Glenn Kubota, "Ascension, Descension," The PEACE 7, no. 12 (January 1992).
[36] "St. Mary's Profile, 2001," 4.
[37] Among the various materials used to assist the parish in articulating its vision for the future and the calling of a new rector were: Episcopal Church Foundation, "Who Are We, the Vestry," The Vestry Resource Guide (New York: The Episcopal Church Foundation/Cornerstone, 2001) and Eric H.F. Law, "Appendix D, Is Your Church Ministry Balanced? The Three-Legged Stool Process," Inclusion: Making

information about what the church was currently doing and the importance of finding ways to reach out to the local community, but there was no clear articulation of an overall mission for the church beyond improving or enhancing current ministries.[38] The profile committee presented a "Profile at a Glance." The vestry's role of articulating the church's vision to provide direction for future ministries was discussed, yet the visioning process seemed stalled. No clear vision for ministry is recorded. Instead, the vestry decided to engage the congregation through a discussion of the future direction for the parish. The responses were disconcerting, reflecting no new ideas or changes. The dominant desire was to grow, to welcome others, to continue to be a multicultural congregation, but not to lose the Japanese American history and identity that was the heritage of the church. The questionnaire, which first had been considered as an open conversation in a meeting, was set down on paper to allow for people to express themselves freely; this was followed up with discussion.

The turning point in the search process came when a long-time clergy member, the Rev. Richard Van Horn, preached a sermon that challenged the congregation to look more deeply into their legacy and build on that instead of staying nostalgically entwined in hopes that could never come to fruition. The call was to remember that the parish's ministry sought to serve immigrants — at that time Japanese immigrants — to find stability and build a life in a new land. He asked: since the community continues to be an immigrant community, what would it look like to seek to serve these immigrants, creating a home, a network of support, a center for cultural education and celebration again?

On April 18, 2010, Father Van Horn led the vestry in a discussion using the questions presented in his sermon and led them through a discussion that culminated with them breaking into four work taskforces, three specific to the future ministry of the parish and the kind of rector they should call to carry out that mission. The first was an "energy audit," to identify what human resources the parish

---

Room for Grace, (St. Louis: Chalice, 2000), 129. The Rev. Canon Joanne Satorius conducted a Mutual Ministry Review on October 30, 2010.

[38] Some examples of things discussed were: the contracting of a musician for the Spanish language service, additional new lectors, a more inclusive directory, installing a handicap ramp, and various community programs and diocesan leadership roles.

had to carry out a new vision in the next five years, the second a "needs audit," to identify the community needs that the church might seek to serve, and the third taskforce, named Mission Recovery Project Dialogues, to explore the past with the older members as a place to build into the future.[39] This process engaged and energized the whole congregation in identifying ways they could support and participate in a forward-looking vision for ministry. The older members were clear that it was time to move forward in new ways. Many members were committed to giving time to live into a new ministry, and finding new ways to do the programs that had been done in the past, programs that supported immigrants. The needs audit identified that the basic needs of the community were issues of survival: employment/jobs, housing, day care and immigration issues/citizen classes. The new priest should have experience and passion for multicultural urban ministry that would build on the parish's heritage and strengths and engage and integrate the community in new ways.

The new rector, the Rev. Anna Olson, was called in the late spring of 2011, her first Sunday being July 24, 2011. Records show that the vestry meetings continued to start with formation discussions. The article "Feasting on Gratitude" was distributed to prepare for stewardship and a discussion of the hopes and plans for parish were discussed. Questions were used to engage in planning, and as information was shared, members were encouraged to reflect on building on the parish's strengths.[40] The parish engaged in discussions and research about possible engagement with the Korean community and collaboration with Holy Trinity, the parish in the adjacent neighborhood.

These discussions remained central at vestry meetings for the next two years, with discussion of research, new possibilities,

---

[39] St. Mary's Church Vestry Minutes, April 18, 2010.
[40] At the August Vestry meeting the handouts were the Sunday, October 2, 2011 reflection from the Episcopal Church's series "Feasting on Gratitude: Stewardship Reflection Series," and the parishes "Vision for St. Mary's and Our New Rector." At the September vestry meeting a planning process was engaged through a series of questions and in October the discussion was about "Making Contact with Our Neighborhood" Initial Steps in Community Connections, where there was discussion of the possibilities of engaging with other local community organizations. There was also discussion about making the church more visible and accessible through signage and banners.

reporting on meetings and conversations with potential partners and collaborators in ministry/service.

Although signage is an ongoing project, the congregation has implemented many of the ideas that developed in their discussions. There has been engagement with the families that work the community garden that has led to the creation of a shrine to Our Lady of Guadalupe. St. Mary's and Holy Trinity have entered into collaborative ministry, sharing staff and services with the contracting of a part-time assistant who also serves the congregation at Holy Trinity. St. Mary's, Holy Trinity and the Korean community at St. James, another episcopal parish in an adjacent neighborhood, have jointly sponsored A Family Fun Day, and are seeking other ways to collaborate. A local education program with local artists has led to beautiful murals in the main entryway to the church complex through the parking lot, and in the parking lot itself. The murals include words and images that incorporate the cultures that make up the parish and the community, outward signs of the welcome being offered to make the congregation the center of the community's life. The music program sponsored by a local Oaxacan community has found a home in the parish, and these various communities have collaborated in cultural celebrations such as The Day of the Dead and Posadas. The cultural and religious celebrations and shared engagement in improving the quality of life of the community are creating a firm foundation for the renewed ministry and mission of this congregation. The education and formation of the leaders is focused on this goal, and the building up of the leaders is building the community, preparing it to live into its call to "seek and serve Christ in all persons."[41]

---

[41] The Episcopal Church, "The Baptismal Covenant," *The Book of Common Prayer* (New York: The Church Hymnal Corporation, 1979), 304-305.

CHAPTER FOUR

Holy Faith Episcopal Church, Inglewood

Case Study

Case Study of Urban Multicultural Congregation #2: The intentionality of Holy Faith's journey into increasing diversity has not been ongoing, affecting its capacity to impact congregational structures.

> As God's house, Holy Faith opens its doors to everyone. God's love is constant, and Holy Faith celebrates the beauty in each one of us because we are all created in God's image. We believe the Holy Spirit embraces, protects, and cares for people of every race, culture, gender, age, sexual orientation, economic circumstance, and belief. Holy Faith respects all people and we welcome everyone to worship with us.

This statement of welcome graces the worship booklet and bulletins of Holy Faith Church in Inglewood, California. It is an amazingly inclusive invitation written by a congregation that is diverse on many levels. The small group discussions that culminated in this articulated vision of community reflected the differences listed.[1] The members of that community were not only women and men, straight, gay, bisexual, poor, working class, middle class and upper middle class, immigrants, educated and semi-illiterate, young and old, they also held different theological, philosophical, and political positions. These differences were secondary to the task at hand—that of defining what they thought church was, what church should be, and what kind of church they wanted to be. In this way the members of the community

---

[1] Holy Faith's multifaceted process of dialogue, education, and reformation of the congregational to become an inclusive multicultural congregation is described in Gary Commins's, *Becoming Bridges: The Spirit and Practice of Diversity* (Cambridge: Cowley Publications, 2007), 137-47.

56

transcended vast differences to worship and work together. They believed that church should be a place where all are welcome, although they could not always perfectly achieve such a welcome. Many who read this statement have joined the church, excited about worshipping in a place that is seeking to live into this challenging vision. For others, the statement has provided the clarity for them to leave, prompted by a statement they consider to be insufficiently orthodox, and put off by the thought of being part of a community that welcomed everyone just as they are.

This statement is distinct from the church's mission statement, which is theologically more circumspect:

The mission of Holy Faith Church is to love and serve Jesus Christ, our Lord and Savior, to promote and support spiritual development and cultural diversity, to worship and share fellowship in God's name, to demonstrate our beliefs by sharing our blessings and faith, and to become advocates of justice and dignity for all people.[2]

In traditional terms the church seeks to serve Christ and promote the gospel, and to serve others in Christ's name, promoting peace and working for justice.[3] Yet this church's intentional commitment to cultural diversity and advocacy distinguishes its mission statement by placing these values at the center of the community's identity and mission.

Holy Faith members participated in a series of study groups, discussions, and activities that set these values intentionally at the center of their corporate life. Like other congregations faced with the inevitable changing context of the urban landscape, Holy Faith went through several stages of transformation from being a white, European American, middle-/upper-middle-class, suburban church, to an integrated parish (African American and European American), and finally to a multicultural, multilingual congregation. The leadership of the congregation at each phase made a commitment to integrate and incorporate new groups from the wider community into the life of the parish. As the landscape of

---

[2] "The Parish of the Holy Faith Episcopal Church, Inglewood, CA, May 2002."
[3] The Episcopal Church, "The Baptismal Covenant," *Book of Common Prayer*, 304-305.

Inglewood and the greater southern Los Angeles area changed, so has the membership of this congregation.

Inglewood, known locally as the City of Champions, is the parish of Holy Faith Episcopal Church. In traditional catholic understandings of parish, the parish is not the church membership but the geographic region in which the church ministers. For Holy Faith Episcopal Church, the City of Inglewood is the primary field of activity. Over the years and with increased mobility, churches draw from an ever wider geographic area. People are not only no longer restricted by parish boundaries to attend a particular church; they also are not primarily identified with particular denominations. Therefore, Holy Faith draws members from throughout the South Los Angeles and South Bay area. There are also members that travel longer distances, from Santa Monica, Culver City, and even as far away as Santa Clarita. Inglewood, a southwest suburb of Los Angeles, has undergone changes that have transformed its identity from a suburb to a city with very "urban" realities and challenges.

The history of Inglewood as a community goes back to the early Mexican settlers. The Centinela Adobe, a historic landmark built in 1834 by Ygnacio Machado, the son of a soldier responsible for protecting early settlers, marks the beginning of the City of Inglewood. The house was a sentinel (Centinela) against marauding pirates, who raided the cattle pastured there by the settlers of Los Angeles. The house was built near the artesian waters (Centinela Springs) that have flowed there since the Ice Age, as evidenced by fossilized remains. That same spring was the center of Indigenous communities, whose artifacts were found when Centinela Park, now Ed Vincent Park, was excavated. Over time, this house was expanded, becoming Rancho Aguaje de Centinela.[4] It was combined with Rancho Sausal Ranando, another land grant, which Sir Robert Burnett of Scotland bought and eventually sold to Daniel Freeman from Canada.[5] This history is significant, not only to the beginnings of Inglewood but also to the identity of Holy Faith Episcopal Church because the church was built as the private chapel of the Freeman family. The church's identity is thus firmly rooted in the beginnings

[4] LAOkay, "Centinela Adobe," Things to do in Los Angeles California, accessed September 27, 2014, http://www.laokay.com/halac/CentinelaAdobe.htm.
[5] City of Inglewood, "City History," Inglewood California, accessed September 27, 2014, http://www.cityofinglewood.org/about/city_history.asp.

of the City of Inglewood, and to this day influences the way some of the parishioners see the role of the church in the City of Inglewood.[6]

Centinela Ranch, with its Centinela Springs, became the home of the Freeman family. Inspired by Charles Nordhoff's "California for Health, Pleasure and Residence: A Book for Travelers and Settlers," Daniel Freeman hoped that the cool breeze would benefit his wife's poor health. The Freeman family built "a vast empire through dry farming, shipping millions of bushels of barley from his wharf at Marina del Rey. Inglewood was the first settlement to be carved out of the 25,000-acre Centinela Ranch in 1888, shortly after a railroad station had been built in the area."[7] That was the same year that the first deputy county clerk and deputy sheriff were appointed. Agriculture would serve as an economic base for the city until World War II; indeed, the high school housed a farm that was an important part of its curriculum.

The agricultural empire was replaced after the financial crash in the early 1900s by the establishment of a Poultry Colony in North Inglewood. Inglewood Park Cemetery was established during that time and soon after a streetcar line serviced it. To this day, Inglewood Park Cemetery is an anchor business in Inglewood. The City was incorporated in 1908 with a population of 1,200, and the earthquake of 1920 put it on the map as a must-see attraction, many who came to visit decided to settle there because of the wonderful climate. From 1920-1925 Inglewood was the fastest growing city in the United States, and became the Chinchilla capital of the world in 1923. The year 1927 saw the beginning of the "Air Age"; Los Angeles leased the Andrew Bennett Ranch and converted it into Mines Field, the predecessor of the Los Angeles International Airport (LAX), the site of the first passenger flight with Charles Lindbergh as the pilot and Will Rogers as the passenger.

In 1932 the Olympics marathon race came through Inglewood, and those games saw three Inglewood High School alum win, beginning the city's identity as the City of Champions. This connection with sports began the city's enduring identity and economic wellbeing; particularly memorable have been the building of The Forum, the home of the Lakers, among other teams, as well

---

[6] Gladys Waddingham, *The History of Inglewood* (Inglewood: The Historical Society of Centinela Valley, 1994), 1-20.
[7] Waddingham, *The History of Inglewood*, 1-20.

as the site of some of the first mass popular music concerts in the country. Although it no longer hosts a professional team, the Forum remains another anchor institution in the City of Inglewood, and with its recent renovations it is again an active entertainment center. In 1938 Hollywood Park was opened (as the Hollywood Park Turf Club). Jack L. Warner (of Warner Brothers) and many other Hollywood notables were original shareholders. Here the famed horse Seabiscuit, among others, won prizes, adding to the image of Inglewood as a City of Champions. Hollywood Park was rebuilt after a fire in 1950 and was expanded in 1972. The Hollywood Park Casino opened in 1994, and there have been other improvements made to the complex over the years.[8] It is another one of the anchor institutions in Inglewood. Thus, throughout the 1990s, Inglewood was a bustling, prosperous town, the center of the aerospace industry, of Hollywood Park entertainment venues, and of various health care facilities.[9]

In common with cities throughout the nation, it is now very much a city that is struggling. The demographics have changed significantly, and there is no longer a dominant industry that supports the city economically. The anchor institutions have joined forces under the name Partners for Progress to maintain a connection to their historical role in the city, and to continue to present the city as a viable and attractive place to live and do business. According to its website, Partners for Progress "is a non-profit marketing cooperative created in 1992 by the city and its largest employers. [Its] mission is to enhance Inglewood's image as an exciting destination for shopping, sports and entertainment, and a world-renowned center for medical services."[10] Yet despite this

---

[8] Hollywood Park, "History of Hollywood Park," Hollywood Park Off-Track Betting OTB, accessed September 29, 2014, http://hollywoodpark.com/about-history.

[9] These and other details are described in Waddingham's, *The History of Inglewood*.

[10] Inglewood Now, "Partners for Progress," accessed March 1, 2012, http://www.inglewoodnow.com/about/index.html now found on Inglewood Chamber of Commerce, accessed September 29, 2014, http://www.inglewoodchamber.com/. This vision has been realized by the City of Inglewood with the building of the SoFi Stadium (2020) and the Intuit Dome (2024) that host the Los Angeles Rams and Chargers in the former and the Los Angeles Clippers in the latter and now make Inglewood a national destination. The extension of light rail train service makes the stadiums and the LAX airport accessible and housing, hotel, and business development has changed the face of the city. A summary of economic

upbeat language, the reality has been one of economic challenges: of high unemployment, of a commercial real estate bubble that hurt businesses, of airlines that suffered both domestically and internationally, and of a higher than average unemployment rate. The motto of the Partners for Progress, *Inglewood City with a Heart*, plays off Centinela Hospital being the home of the Tommy Lasorda Heart Institute, a legendary cardiac care facility. [11] The development projects discussed on the website are the three shopping centers that were developed after the attempt to revitalize the Historic Market Street Shopping District did not succeed. Many of the "mom and pop stores" located there clearly cater to a lower income crowd. There is a sporting goods store (Big Five), and it is the center of school uniform shopping with one of the largest stores in the area still doing good business (Michael's). The newer shopping centers are all adjacent to each other on Century Boulevard.

The hospitals also reflect the challenges urban areas face. The city continues to tout its medical facilities, yet Daniel Freeman Memorial Hospital has been closed. When the emergency room closed in 2006, at a time when hospital emergency room closings were epidemic in the Southern Los Angeles County area,[12] both King-Drew Medical Center and R.F. Kennedy Medical Center emergency rooms had also recently closed. The hospital has also faced labor issues. Prime Healthcare Hospitals were resistant to signing a neutrality agreement with SEIU (Service Employees International Union). Worker's contract negotiations were also a theme of several City Council meetings.[13] Almost all the meetings of 2010 were conducted in closed sessions as the city negotiated

---

development projects can be found on the city's website https://www.cityofinglewood.org/1499/Projects-in-the-Pipeline (accessed February 24, 2025).

[11] "Tommy Lasorda Heart Institute," Centinela Hospital Medical Center, accessed September 28, 2014, http://www.centinelamed.com/Our_Services/Tommy_Lasorda_Heart_Institute.html.

[12] Data Desk, "California's Hospitals Emergency Room Closures," *Los Angeles Times*, A Tribune Newspaper website, accessed September 28, 2014, http://projects.latimes.com/hospitals/emergency-rooms/no/closed/list.

[13] Inglewood City Council, "City Council Minutes," City of Inglewood California, accessed September 28, 2014, http://www.cityofinglewood.org/city_hall/city_council/min/ccm/2010_minutes.asp.

worker issues and contracts. Issues of gang violence, police brutality, and racial/ethnic tensions in the school have also been challenges that Inglewood has in common with many urban centers.

The 2010 Census provides a good overall picture of the community. In 2010 Inglewood had a population of 109,673 and it projected growth to 111,542 by 2013. Inglewood is 47.5% male and 52.5% female, with a median age of 33.4 years. Between 2000 and 2010, the Latino population grew from 46% to 50.6%, the dominant cultural group being Mexicans at 38.3% of the Latino population. African Americans/Blacks are 43.9% of the population and Whites (European Americans) make up 23.3% of the population. The majority of the inhabitants are renters (63% vs. 37% home owners), with an average household size of 2.97 people. Of the population, 72.7% were born in the United States and its territories. Of the foreign born 27.3%, the vast majority (90.1%) was born in Latin America. Of these, 45.7% speak Spanish in the home, and 50% speak only English. The unemployment rate is 12.5%, with 33.7% of those over sixteen years of age not in the labor force (including the retired). The majority of those employed are in occupations other than manual labor, construction, maintenance, production, and transportation. In total, 27.9% are in sales and office occupations, 25.6% are in service occupations, and 23.5% are in management, business, science, and arts occupations. The majority (74%) are private wage and salary workers, and the top five industries represented are education, health care, and social assistance at 20.3%, professional, scientific and management, analytical, administrative and waste management services at 11.7%, arts, entertainment and recreation, and accommodation and food services at 10.9%, retail trade at 9.9%, and transportation, warehousing, and utilities at 9.5%. The median household income is $44, 558 and the mean is $58,328. A total of 25.6% of the population does not have health insurance, and the income of 20.1% of the city's population is below the poverty level. Other significant social characteristics are that 30.2% of grandparents are living with and responsible for the care of their grandchildren, that 72.1% of the population have completed a high school education or above, and that 17.7% have completed a Bachelor's degree or higher.[14]

---

[14] U. S. Census Bureau, "American Fact Finder," accessed September 25, 2014, http://factfinder2.census.gov/faces/nav/jsf/pages/community_facts.xhtml.

The political power base is shifting to match these demographics. In the most recent election, the city council went from being predominantly Black, with one Latino representative among four council members, to electing a second Latino council member, which made the city council 50% Black and 50% Latino. The four City Council members reflect the city's history and future. Indeed, the Council recently lost its one European American/white female city council member, who had served for seventeen years.[15] The current mayor is a law-and-order candidate, who previously served twenty years on the Inglewood Police Force, rising from officer to Deputy Chief of Police; he has been Chief of Police for the City of Santa Monica for the last ten years. His predecessor was "Hanging" Judge Roosevelt Dorn, who was removed from office and convicted of impropriety, with a temporary interim term served by Daniel Tabor, a lifelong resident and community organizer, who subsequently failed to win election to a full term. The mayors of Inglewood have been African American since 1984 when Edward Vincent, a former football star, was elected its first Black mayor. There is a large base of retired and current union members. There are many Black churches that historically have had good connections to city government and to the business leaders of the Chamber of Commerce. There is an active ministerial association, primarily male, primarily Black, and primarily conservative (not too long ago there was a question as to whether a woman could become a member; many did not "believe in" women ministers).

With this historical and civic background in mind, Holy Faith's stance as a welcoming parish that seeks to involve and integrate people from a variety of communities, customs, cultures, and languages has set it ahead of the City of Inglewood, where power has only recently begun to be shared in a way that reflects the demographic makeup of the city. The progress towards the goal of

---

[15] Alex Padilla unseated 20-year incumbent Judy Dunlap to shift the composition of the city council of 5 to 2 African Americans, 2 Latinos and the African American Mayor. "Dotson Padilla Win in Inglewood," *Los Angeles Wave Newspaper*, accessed September 20, 2014, http://wavenewspapers.com/news/local/west_edition/article_802fb548-d3c7-11e2-bd4d-001a4bcf6878.html and "Inglewood Elections," *The Sentinel*, accessed September 20, 2014, http://www.lasentinel.net/index.php?option=com_content&view=article&id=10 813:inglewood-elections&catid=80&Itemid=170.

full inclusion has not been without its challenges. Ken Adams, a centenarian whose family was one of the first Black families to join Holy Faith, saw his involvement in the congregation as an extension of his work for civil rights for African Americans. Ken was involved in the Civil Rights Movement of the '50s and '60s and marched with Dr. Martin L. King, Jr. in Chicago. He joined the parish in the late '60s and the presence of his family made it possible subsequently for other families to join without being the "only ones."[16] The African American members of the congregation became more numerous with the arrival of the Rev. Gary Commins as rector; thanks to his commitment to fight racism and the work he did to increase awareness of racial issues, the congregation has become a catalyst for anti-racism projects throughout the diocese.[17]

In the early 1990's members of Holy Faith Episcopal Church participated in a variety of discussion sessions and workshops that sought to facilitate the process of becoming more diverse and inclusive as part of its mission to work for justice. They participated in The White Racial Awareness Process to deal with issues of race among the white members of the congregation, as well as other workshops on matters of race, class, culture, gender, and sexual orientation. Subsequently this workshop model to educate and empower was offered to other congregations in the Diocese of Los Angeles interested in similar anti-racism and inclusion work.[18] The Episcopal Peace and Justice Network in collaboration with The National Conference eventually published *The White Racial Awareness Process*, making it available for broad use.

In recent years, persons of Latin American origin and descent began to move into Inglewood in greater and greater numbers. In 1993 the parish began to offer a worship service in Spanish to welcome this part of the Inglewood community.[19] Classes were offered in English as a Second Language, which allowed many

---

16 Spellers, *Radical Welcome*, 84-85.
17 The Cultural Diversity Commission working with the Outreach Commission took the experience of the parish dialogues (described in Commins, *Becoming Bridges*) and offered trainings and sessions for parishes in the Diocese of Los Angeles. Their process, in collaboration with other racial justice organizations, is documented in: Episcopal Peace and Justice Network, *White Racial Awareness Process: The Episcopal Church Facilitator Guidelines* (Salem, N.J.: New Earth, 1993).
18 Episcopal Peace and Justice Network, *White Racial Awareness Process*.
19 Waddingham, *The History of Inglewood*, 89.

people to become more fluent, able to improve their opportunities of employment and survival, as well as supporting their interest in becoming citizens of the United States. Classes were also offered in Spanish, so that English-speaking members interested in more interaction with their Spanish-speaking neighbors could learn their language.

In addition to such educational programs, structural changes introduced to the parish began to make the institutional culture more inclusive. The vestry was racially and ethnically mixed and a Cultural Diversity Committee was established to plan and implement events and activities, in collaboration with other church committees, that would increase cross cultural learning and interaction. These events ranged from discussion groups and study to cultural celebrations, such as African Sunday and Holy Faith Day on which persons brought food and cultural artifacts that reflected their culture. The language classes offered increased the number of bilingual persons in the congregation. The liturgy was also changed to include practices, hymnody, and prayer that reflected the various cultures present in the congregation and the values of inclusion that were becoming a central part of the parish's identity. The church regularly incorporated an "African Offertory Procession" in which members brought the offerings of the congregation to the altar with song, dance, and praise. The church changed its liturgical language to be more inclusive, collected music from the various cultures into a booklet then regularly used for worship, and eventually translated songs and offered worship in the three dominant languages of the congregation, English, Spanish and Igbo.

The church also offered ministries that welcomed and sought to minister to the needs of the community. Although Holy Faith itself is located in a stable, high-income neighborhood, poverty, violence, and health disparities were well represented in the broader city. A food bank program at the church sought to address some of the challenges faced daily by many working poor families whose heads of households held full-time employment but whose income was insufficient to cover all basic living expenses.

The parish furthermore offers a youth program called Alternatives to Violence, which seeks to address the race and gang related violence taking place in schools. Young people were first invited and eventually referred by the juvenile justice system and local high schools to come and learn peacemaking skills. The series of workshops and discussion sessions taught the young people problem solving, communication skills, stress management, and mediation skills that they could use on their high school campuses. The program had a self-care component that addressed health issues such as nutrition, exercise, and the impact of drugs and alcohol. Young people worked on community projects to promote peace and well-being in the community, projects such as graffiti removal and mural creation, gardening, and workshops at their schools. Young people led in sharing the skills and strategies for non-violent conflict resolution and community peacemaking. This program was eventually invited into the Inglewood schools. Through assembly presentations, skits, classroom workshops, and school-wide community projects, young people and their adult mentors, Lloyd Wilkey and Pam Cysner, the program directors, promoted respect of different cultural groups, intercultural dialogue, and peacemaking within the schools and by extension throughout the community. The school district also asked Wilkey and Cysner to offer these workshops to school leaders; the pair has since led many cultural sensitivity and diversity training workshops and retreats for community-based organizations throughout Los Angeles County.[20]

Holy Faith's experience and work made it the site of leadership development that impacted the broader church. The Episcopal Urban Internship Program was founded in 1994 as a program of the Diocese of Los Angeles, and it brought young people together to live a year in intentional Christian community and service in Los Angeles County. For many young people it was a year of discernment and formation, a year in which they garnered experience working in social service agencies and learning and reflecting on issues of oppression and justice. The young people lived in Holy Faith's rectory, participated in worship, and

---

[20] This program, which was initially developed in response to the Los Angeles Civil Unrest, continues to provide youth leadership development programing and was featured on public radio KPCC. Grant Slater, "Boxing mentor 'The LA Riot' Seeks a Different Kind of Uprising," Southern California Public Radio, April 30, 2012, accessed September 20, 2014, http://www.scpr.org/news/2012/04/30/32247/boxing-mentor-who-calls-himself-la-riot-seeks-diff/, more information can be found on the organization's Facebook, LA Riot Boxing, accessed September 25, 2014, https://www.facebook.com/LARiotBoxing.

participated in the ministries of the congregation. The other leadership development program that grew out of Holy Faith's intentional work on multicultural ministry was an intercession course offered for seminarians on Multicultural Ministry. Seminary students spent the month of January living with a Holy Faith host family, participating in worship, and meeting with leaders of the different Episcopal congregations engaged in multicultural ministries in the Diocese of Los Angeles. These conversations, informed by readings, provided students with opportunities to learn about the various ways that multicultural ministry was being done in a very diverse context. Discussion with actual practitioners and leaders of these congregations allowed for questions and concerns to be explored contextually, as each site shared with them its experience in trying to build an inclusive, multicultural church. This was an investment in the future leadership of the broader church, and an opportunity for the congregational leaders themselves to reflect on their experiences as they shared the good news of what ministry can look like when congregations cross lines of difference.

The outreach committee of the Holy Faith parish collaborated, designed, and developed these and additional programs that addressed needs in the community. The committee opened an afterschool program and procured a van through a grant from the United Thank Offering of the Episcopal Church Women. Leaders of this program picked up elementary school-aged children after school and brought them to the parish hall where leaders helped them with homework and provided supervised play and healthy snacks. This provided academic support, but also a safe place for children while parents were at work. Over the course of several summers, this program took various forms: a sports camp, nutrition and fitness programming for children and their families, healthy cooking classes for those who came to the food bank using the food available there, and workshops on the issues that disproportionately impact the health of Black and Latino families: hypertension, diabetes, HIV/AIDS, heart disease, lung disease, and sickle cell anemia. Eventually local schools began to provide afterschool programs, right around the time that grant funding ended for the church, and the afterschool program was discontinued.

The programs that addressed the health disparities in the congregation evolved over the years. State and Federal grants provided the resources for nutrition, exercise, and health education workshops. Other congregations echoed the need for such programs. Since Holy Faith congregation could not sustain these programs on their own over the long term, three other urban congregations engaged in similar projects joined with Holy Faith to form a 501(c)3 non-profit organization, The Jubilee Consortium, dedicated to health programming, specifically nutrition and fitness programs for Latino and African American children and adults. Likewise, the Alternatives to Violence program expanded to other congregations in collaboration with the Jubilee Consortium, and together they developed other programming designed to address the particular needs and interests of each community. The Episcopal Urban Intern Program has also grown and become incorporated into the Jubilee Consortium's work. The Jubilee Consortium currently hosts various programs around the greater Los Angeles area that address community health, leadership development, and health advocacy.[21]

These efforts to promote health for children and their families led members of Holy Faith to become community advocates for health and wellness. Holy Faith leadership participated in community meetings for the redevelopment of the Market Street shopping area, bringing a Farmer's Market to Inglewood, addressing police brutality charges, and becoming involved in other larger campaigns. They participated in organizing efforts on issues of health with the Community Health Councils and sought to address the closure of Daniel Freeman hospital. When the hospital closure could not be prevented, they joined the fight to keep open the YWCA fitness center on the hospital grounds for the seniors who had been using it as part of their physical rehabilitation and health maintenance. This extended the life of this important low-cost resource in the community. Parishioners and church leadership also became involved in supporting workers seeking better working conditions for themselves and their families. Holy Faith Church was active in the Los Angeles Living Wage Campaign and in supporting the hotel workers at Los Angeles International Airport when they

---

[21] Jubilee Consortium, accessed September 27, 2014, http://www.jubileeconsortium.org/about/mission/.

sought to win a contract. At one particular hotel, one of the few union hotels on the Century Boulevard strip by the airport, longtime workers were fired because of their organizing efforts. Holy Faith led and participated in weekly prayer vigils that were held at the hotel to draw attention to the injustice that had been perpetrated. As a result, some of the workers were rehired while others went on to provide leadership at other hotels in the Los Angeles area. In all of these ways members of the church lived out their belief in justice, equality, and the respect and dignity of persons within and without the walls of the church through parish programming and on the streets of their community.

The intentional training of facilitators in the White Racial Awareness Program (WRAP), the establishment of two parish commissions that worked on issues of welcome, inclusion, and ministry (the Outreach and the Cultural Awareness), and the discussion series, were all opportunities for intentional lay leadership development for people committed to inclusive, diverse congregations. The training sessions explored issues of cultural history and difference, experiences of oppression and privilege, and structural and systemic power and abuse of power. As members raised issues in the congregation, they explored and discussed new issues. Discussions of full inclusion of lesbian, gay, bisexual, and transgender persons at church and at all levels of leadership in the church began a dialogue on an issue that was difficult given the theological differences represented in the congregation. The welcome statement shows that the decision to welcome and respect all people was the starting point on issues that would have to be part of a longer-term ongoing conversation. These conversations at Holy Faith reflected the conversation that was taking place in the wider Church.

Although the leadership of the congregation was fully engaged in these processes, there were many members who were on the margins of these discussions and learning opportunities. Living with the tension of disagreement and taking a live-and-let-live attitude was enough for polite exchanges in the parish, but the decision of the 2003 General Convention of the Episcopal Church to ratify the election of (openly gay and partnered) Bishop Gene Robinson of New Hampshire caused some people on the margins of these discussions to take offense and depart from the congregation. As the newly installed rector of Holy Faith, I served as a deputy to that General Convention and had spoken in support of the resolution to ratify the election of Gene Robinson. Although most members agreed that everyone should be welcome in church, they still held to the traditional teaching of homosexuality as sin that they were taught as children. A significant number of the Nigerian members decided to leave the congregation in response to Archbishop Akinola's call for Nigerians to leave the Episcopal Church in protest of the ratification of Gene Robinson's election.[22] But it was not only Nigerian members who departed but also others who felt that bishops should be held to a higher standard, that by virtue of their office and leadership role in the church homosexuals called to the office of bishop should sacrifice and remain celibate. These theological differences had long co-existed at Holy Faith but this action of the General Convention brought the differences of opinion to a head and some members were no longer willing theologically to accept such inclusion. It is possible that if these persons had engaged more fully in the conversations taking place at the church, they might have been able to find a way to live with both values, although they were in tension.

Including a greater number of people into discussions, study, and dialogue to allow for a deeper commitment to inclusion, and to examine long held theological and cultural beliefs is a challenge in every congregation. Though leaders and active members engage in formation programs, many people only participate in Sunday worship, where exposure to theological reflections on controversial topics may occur but in-depth engagement with them rarely happens, especially not the kind of engagement that fosters change, the kind of discussion with others in the community in which long held positions can be amicably challenged.

In addition to the Nigerian members who left because of the consecration of Gene Robinson as Bishop of New Hampshire, other members also left Holy Faith in the years between 2003-2005. Some members left during the interim period and some upon the calling of a woman to serve as rector. Although women had served as assistants to the rector in the past, a few members felt that women

---

[22] James Solheim, "International Reaction to Gene Robinson's Consecration in New Hampshire Mixed," *Anglican Communion News Service*, November 6, 2003, accessed September 25, 2014, http://www.anglicannews.org/news/2003/11/international-reaction-to-gene-robinsons-consecration-in-new-hampshire-mixed.aspx.

should not serve "over" the congregation as senior pastor. Other members left because they were not in agreement with the mission emphasis on multicultural inclusivity, and this coincided with the call of a new dynamic clergyperson at the parish in their own neighborhoods. Families decided to join the churches that were closer to them geographically. The Holy Faith congregation had included many families that travelled 3-15 miles to worship at Holy Faith, passing multiple Episcopal churches on the way. Some of these families had once lived in Inglewood when they first joined the church, but as their families grew and they purchased affordable homes outside of the South Los Angeles area, these families traveled great distances to continue to be a part of the parish. As children grew up and parents became interested in them being more active in the church and the community, these families began to identify and attend congregations closer to their homes. Some went to other Episcopal churches and others to non-denominational and evangelical congregations with more traditional theologies. Others left because their class assumptions of the kind of programs the church should have for their children were not being fulfilled at Holy Faith, such as age specific Sunday School programs. Yet there were also new additions to the congregation, families and individuals that were attracted to the inclusive mission and worship that Holy Faith was adopting.

The loss of these families was hard on the congregation. Many of those who left, who were almost all people who did not live in Inglewood, had been in leadership positions in the congregation. They were people who had served on the vestry and on the search committee for the rector. They populated the committees that were vital to the day-to-day work of the church—choir, altar guild, finance, and administration—and this vacuum of leadership made maintenance of the congregation difficult. There was an increased reliance on staff at a time when staff time was being reduced because of ongoing financial challenges. This issue of finances would later come to a head when it was discovered that the parish administrator, a hard-working person who had taken on many of the responsibilities left vacant, had embezzled from the church throughout his tenure of seven years.

The work of being a vital, multicultural congregation engaged with the wider community is ongoing, ever-evolving work. Holy Faith has lived into this identity for many years. It has seen itself as a multicultural community in God's service, and this identity has deepened as they have sought not only to welcome the other, but also to continue to be transformed by the other. This ongoing process has led to the congregation's own continual transformation. Ongoing visioning has become the means for this congregation's renewal. In 2007 the congregation once again engaged a process of discussion and reflection.[23] The goal was to engage the congregation in visioning for the next five years. The congregation asked itself: What new thing is God calling Holy Faith to do? The vestry process, led by an outside facilitator with experience in working with urban churches, provided the opportunity for the vestry members to share their faith stories by reflecting on Scripture and on their experience of communal life at Holy Faith. Remembering and sharing their reasons for coming and staying to be part of the community helped the group identify the strengths and the positive experiences that were an indication of God's activity in their lives. These reflections and memories became the basis for an exploration of the gifts they have to share with the community they are called to serve. The church leaders also participated in community walk-around. They were invited to take notes regarding what they saw in their community: What businesses were operating? What did their neighbors look like? What were they engaged in? Were they shopping? Were they traveling with small children? Were they elderly people being transported? These questions led to an increased awareness of who exactly it was they were seeking to welcome and serve, what the programs and activities might be that would respond to the actual needs of the community residents, and what might lead those residents to become involved in the congregation. The leadership then facilitated a similar process with members of the congregation. The remnant at Holy Faith along with the new families met in small groups to discuss what they enjoyed about being at Holy Faith and what kinds of programs they wanted to see happening at the church. Discussing the assets of the congregation, both in terms of past history and present gifts and interests led to the creation of a list that built on the best of the

---

[23] The parish consulted with an urban strategist of the Methodist Church. For a year they met, studied, and discussed church growth and community outreach to respond to the priority of church growth that had been set by the vestry. The vestry minutes summarize these sessions and the tasks they performed and reviewed as part of this learning process.

congregation's past to make the vision of the future possible. Although not a formal appreciative inquiry process, the discussions were nonetheless built on those same principles.[24]

The result of these conversations was a continued commitment to be an inclusive, justice-seeking community. There was also great interest in finding ways to welcome the broader community and their concerns into the life of the church. Priorities were identified for making changes that would make the church more accessible and responsive to the community. The list is familiar: further adaptations to the worship service so that it was more inclusive of the cultures of the people of color that reflect the demographics of Inglewood; programming for young people especially Latino, African American, and biracial/bicultural young people—the fastest growing demographic in Inglewood; and multigenerational and multicultural activities that foster community amongst church members and the wider community, especially between members of different cultural communities.

The church initiated programs and activities based on this conversation/reflection process. It made more changes to the liturgy, established an updated canon of music, which led eventually to the music leaders composing a Latin Salsa Mass setting, *Misa del Son*. The "Faithful Band" also held a concert that promoted several musical talents including music that had been written specifically for the congregation on the occasion of its centennial, and reflected its values of inclusion and justice. The main service became bilingual and multicultural, and the format of the sermons became more educational and interactive. There had been a great interest expressed in Bible Study and small group interaction, yet the schedule of the members made this prohibitive. Making the sermon time more interactive, both with dialogue sermons and with opportunities to reflect on questions in small groups, allowed for some of this experience to be shared during the time all committed to be present, Sunday mornings. This use of didactic, dialogue sermons, and small group conversations during the service allowed everyone to be engaged in the discussion, no longer leaving up to chance whether the members of the

---

[24] Mark Lau Branson, *Memories, Hopes and Conversations: Appreciative Inquiry and Congregational Change* (Herdon, Virginia: The Alban Institute, 2004). This text documents a similar process, asking similar questions, conducted with a congregation seeking to engage and incorporate the community beyond its doors.

congregation would participate in the discussion of theology, church teaching, and God's call upon their lives.

The church also set up game nights on which people gathered, shared food, and played a variety of board games. These events were multigenerational and multicultural, and provided free opportunities for fun and engagement. In addition, thanks to the involvement of a parishioner and the increased collaboration with *9 to 5*, the non-profit organization that works to change unjust working conditions for women, Holy Faith became the regular venue for their movie nights and discussions. This was another opportunity for community and church members to interact over food, movies, and discussions on issues of justice for women workers.

Two other issues identified were also made priorities, especially for the centennial celebrations: increased attention to communication and promotion of events, and continued improvements to the church buildings and grounds. Generous donations by several church members allowed the most urgent issues of deferred maintenance to be addressed and the centennial year celebrations ended with a banquet held on the church grounds, to celebrate new landscaping and church doors, updated gas lines, and other repairs. These building repairs and improvements allowed the church to capitalize and invest in one of its greatest assets, the buildings and grounds. The church provides space for non-profit and volunteer organizations that work on community issues, as well as a safe space for community members to have family celebrations. This is another way of the church sharing the gifts it has with community members that need them, and in so doing using and developing resources for continuing ministry.

New leadership slowly emerged, as newer families took on responsibilities and worked to implement these new programs. The centennial celebrations focused on a series of activities that would both raise funds and raise fun, providing enjoyable opportunities for families to engage each other and get to know each other better. The work of the committee solidified a new set of leaders that had already taken the lead on many things, but working together on the centennial celebrations allowed friendships to develop as well.

It was also during the centennial that the church discovered the embezzlement. This meant that the next year was spent in investigation and recovery of lost assets. The parish administrator responsible was eventually arrested and sentenced. The leadership worked in overdrive to find and organize the evidence and then set up systems that would ensure that accountability was sustained in future. Although many checks and balances had already been in place, the administrator, having worked at a bank, had managed to devise a very elaborate system to embezzle the funds. It became apparent that more people needed to be involved in keeping things running, especially as regards finances, and that the tendency in non-profit organizations to trust the person who is willing to carry an undue burden had made this organization vulnerable.

These major challenges in the church's life point to two important aspects of leadership development that need to be addressed when working in these contexts. Urban congregations, especially those with limited resources, must deal with the high rate of mobility of its membership and the need to operate with limited volunteer resources to sustain an under-resourced organization. The ability to continually incorporate new members, engage them in ways that encourage commitment, and then involve them as volunteers in the activities that sustain the organization administratively and programmatically is a continual challenge. This makes leadership formation and development a priority of ministry in the urban parish. This reality challenges the dominant understanding of many current churchgoers. In this model discipleship is central.[25] This model, in addition to being a biblical one, provides push back to the entertainment and/or chaplaincy conceptions of worship and pastoral care. The centrality of inspiring worship and spiritual care and counseling in the ministry of the Christian church cannot be underestimated. Yet the gospel imperative has always been that we "go forth and do likewise." Gospel encounters with Jesus not only led to healing in body, mind, and spirit but each person then went forth to minister and serve another. Jesus' disciples, the named and the unnamed, became the people who went forth, shared the good news, and resourced the ministry through their work and finances.

Discipleship and leadership development continue to be essential in urban ministry today. This becomes more essential as

---

[25] The model assumed by Greenway in *Discipling in the City*, is that the goal of ministry and the mission of the church is to make disciples of all people, "The Great Commission" as found in Matthew 28:19.

the middle-class model of ministry of having one professional clergy person for each parish is no longer viable in a society with a shrinking middle class. The social factors that mitigate against the institutional corporate model of mainline denominations require urban ministries to find other models for long-term sustainability. In order for calls to ministry to be more nimble and responsive, churches do well to assume a posture more consistent with people's movements than with corporate institutions. A study on the ability to use the resources at hand and leverage them for the economic resources necessary to sustain congregational life[26] is beyond the scope of this particular text; suffice it to say here that such work must be paired with constant development of human resources— the formation, development, and support of the lay people of the church.

In order to continuously develop leaders in organizations that are highly mobile, formation needs to be seen as part of the ongoing mission and functioning of the church, not a program that is offered once or twice a year. Each aspect of congregational life must emphasize the centrality of learning, practice, and reflection as essential to living out the mission of the church. The pastoral cycle of theological reflection: "see, judge, act" or experience, analysis, prayerful reflection, and pastoral action, must be incorporated at every level of ministry in the church.[27] This model of Christian formation has been identified as important for the urban church: every aspect and every person is involved in the process of congregational formation.[28]

The awareness developed through the educational opportunities offered at Holy Faith, as it worked at becoming multicultural was good for those members present. However, those who did not participate remained at the margins. New members

---

[26] See Eric H.F. Law, *Holy Currencies: Six Blessings for Sustainable Missional Ministries* (St. Louis: Chalice, 2013), for a discussion of ways that congregations can build on their assets to become sustainable.

[27] The pastoral reflection cycle is often used to describe a process of learning that is grounded in action and reflection. This model is the basis of Freire's liberative pedagogy and practical theologians use it as a framework for theological reflection. A good summary of this pedagogical model and its use by Thomas H. Groome in religious education/formation can be found in Moore's *Teaching from the Heart*, 171-3.

[28] Letty Russell offers an integrative congregational religious education program in an essay in Rogers, *Urban Church Education*, 30.

who joined the church, attracted by the multicultural identity of the church, also did not participate in the educational programs that had led to this transformation, and therefore did not necessarily have the skills to participate fully or to become leaders who were aware and intentional about the need to operate in a way that consistently sought to incorporate difference. The assumption that this was the culture of the church went but so far. In every culture there must be mechanisms by which to pass the culture on to the next generation. The process of socialization occurs through living within the community, but also through intentional practices, rituals, and rites that form and integrate the next generation. The organization must be a learning organization, where risk and growth are a part of the way things are done.[29]

This type of formation is also indicated when dealing with the pernicious issues of oppression. The multivalent and the structural nature of power and oppression in society also calls for ongoing opportunities for reflection, study, and dialogue. This is well reflected in the congregations that made a commitment to being multiracial in *A House of Prayer for all Peoples*.[30] In each of the cases presented the congregations continued to offer discussion groups, workshops, and ongoing study sessions to continue to support the membership with opportunities to work in a sustained way on issues of racism and oppression. Some of the congregation found ways to integrate new members into existing study groups while maintaining a "safe" space for having difficult conversations.

This aspect of formation was missing in the model of leadership formation practiced at Holy Faith. The programs and sessions that happened occurred more in keeping with an annual or biannual effort at leadership development as different members of the congregation were integrated into various ministries. Bigger visioning processes happened every five years. Although this kept the parish asking the questions about ministry that keep the parish vital, there is an overreliance on the clergy leadership to continue to interpret and educate around issues of systemic oppression and the appropriate Christian response. Sunday sermons became the primary way that people engaged these topics, as opposed to

---

[29] See Peter Senge, *The Fifth Discipline, The Art and Practice of the Learning Organization* (New York: Doubleday/Currency, 1990) for a discussion of learning organizations.
[30] Kujawa-Holbrook, *A House of Prayer for All Peoples*.

engaging as a community in a process of sharing their own lived experiences about these topics, analyzing their experience together, and then in prayerful theological reflection with the tradition (scripture, church teaching, liturgical practices) coming together to create a response, an action that sought to address the injustice, exclusion, and oppression that they had identified. This missing element limits the depth with which these issues are engaged regularly, with the result that the culture of the institution is not consistently being formed by the experiences of the lay people and specifically the lay leaders. Instead, the clergy are providing material for reflection that keeps the issues distant and intellectual, not something which the congregation is called to integrate into their lives at all levels and to act upon with their own gifts and strengths. Incorporating learning experiences at all levels of communal life and then finding opportunities for reflection and discussion must therefore become the goal and is something that critical/liberative pedagogies provide. Such a liberative pedagogy would transform each individual and the institution in an ongoing way, and would integrate new members not just into what the congregation seeks to be, but also in how they as part of the congregation are engaged in making this a sustainable reality.

The linear model of holding a series of discussions to consider a particular issue does not take into account the time it takes to fully understand and consider the complex ways that issues of race, class, gender, sexual identity and orientation, physical and mental abilities and challenges intersect nor of the cultures that each of these social constructs embodies and informs. To welcome the other and to be transformed by the other requires intentional reflection on self and others with a critical eye towards the institutions that support and limit human development. To reflect on the value that each person brings as gifts for ministry through their experience and knowledge requires that these be examined and incorporated by as many people as possible. Clergy highlighting these issues and bringing them forth for reflection in a sermon or a vestry meeting reflection time should only be one part of a multivalent formation process that seeks to address a complex learning context. Pedagogical strategies of Critical Multicultural Education can be applied to the context of the parish so that each event, meeting, activity and program is designed to be a part of an ongoing process of reflecting on experience, with analytical tools that allow for an appropriate and organic theological, ministerial response on the part of all the body of Christ, the whole congregation, and especially the lay leadership.

How can the regular times of gathering — committee meetings, vestry meetings, social/coffee hour, worship, Sunday School, Bible Study, social action activities, pastoral/service activities, and personal spiritual practices — become opportunities for continued critical learning? How might such times and such learning be incorporated into a context that already struggles with limited resources of people, time, and finances? An analysis of the elements of critical multicultural education and the ways they can be incorporated in a congregational setting may provide some ideas of how this ongoing process of critical reflection and engagement can become part of the culture of the church as a learning organization.

CHAPTER FIVE

Analysis and Reflection

Rooted in the progressive educational tradition, critical multicultural pedagogy advances Dewey's understanding of the purpose of education. That is, it equips people to be active, positive contributors to society, and it is essential for a good democracy. Each person must be able to read and reason, to engage in discussion, and to form an opinion that contributes to the ordering of society. Participation in civil government—voting, holding legislators accountable, contributing through work for the good of the whole—are learned skills, and education is the way to build this capacity in a democratic society. This understanding is operative in Albert Coe's religious education writings, and critical pedagogies that seek to develop conscientization and praxis for justice take these concepts a step further.

In this context, Paolo Freire's work was revolutionary. It took seriously Dewey's goal of education as a process of formation whose goal is empowerment and democratic engagement, but it also went further, developing a pedagogy of the oppressed, a methodology that practiced these principles of empowerment and democratic engagement in the educational process itself, rather than seeing those simply as a possible *result* of education. Fundamentally, it understood that both students and teachers are engaged in a learning process. Students have experiences that inform their understanding of their society, its needs, and the injustices that need to be remedied. When students' existing knowledge and experience is engaged and built upon, the learning is contextualized and students become aware of their role as creators of culture rather than just as passive inheritors of it.[1] Conscientization, the process of

---

[1] Paulo Freire, *Pedagogy of the Oppressed: 30th Anniversary Edition* (New York: Continuum, 2005). This pedagogy applied to literacy education in Brazil has been

culture making described and utilized by Freire for literacy education in Brazil, is a process of understanding the context in which one is living, the present historical moment. Through this awareness each person recognizes him or herself as a subject of history and not merely an object in it. This awareness, and the problematizing of it led by the facilitator (teacher), ideally lead both student and teacher to question the present historical moment and to begin to see how systems and institutions that oppress can be challenged and changed to liberate. Learners, both student and teachers, do this through an analysis of the context, the historical moment, and an analysis of the power they can access and bring to bear to effect change in their oppressive situation. They become aware of the power they have to change their circumstances, and see in education the tools that will allow them to access and affect the system.

This process of analysis and reflection that leads to conscientization is important for congregational leaders faced with challenging and changing their internal structures and finding ways to have a positive impact in their communities. Reflecting on and analyzing their experience and their context can lead to questioning the status quo and strategizing action/praxis to effect change that will improve the quality of life of their community. For congregational leaders, the communal reality that needs to be problematized is both in the congregation and in the neighborhood. Transforming the congregation, so that it is a welcoming and just community, means analyzing the systems and structures already operative within the congregation. The leadership must be conscientized to see itself as called to a ministry for justice, a ministry that seeks change within and without the church.

The pedagogical framework of action-reflection utilized in critical pedagogies and liberation theologies is the most appropriate one for leadership development in urban congregations. Congregations faced with the challenge of change (which arguably all are) require an ongoing practice of learning that allows them to reflect on their activity and act on their reflections. Branson and Lau describe this "pastoral cycle" as the work of practical theology that

---

the launching point for many liberative projects that seek to engage the student and the educational project as one of conscientization, politicization, and praxis for social transformation.

congregational leaders must engage to be intentionally multicultural.[2] This assumes that congregations are not just seeking to have people of different racial, ethnic, and class groups join their congregations to create an optic of inclusion, but rather that congregations are responding to the gospel call for churches to engage people across lines of difference in a way that promotes justice and shows the love and care that each believer is called to express and live into with the "other."

Reflection on action is central to learning and leadership development.[3] Many congregations seek to reach out or serve their neighbors without having questioned the contexts to which they are inviting people, or the reasons service is necessary. The assumptions of welcome and service need to be problematized in order to be truly responsive and to engage the context and the lived reality of the community. Engaging the pastoral reflection circle facilitates analysis and thoughtful interaction with the systems at play. Taking the time to reflect on their action, to analyze the structures they are seeking to impact, and the communities they are seeking to serve, these are all crucial steps in the process. Without such steps, the activity of inclusion can easily become an end in itself, not a part of the ongoing ministry, practice, and transformation of the congregation. Hit-or-miss activities and changes can lead to congregational burnout, because they are not responsive to the actual needs of the community or to the actual systems that are maintaining the current situation in need of adjustment. When nothing changes, leaders understandably often feel that they have attempted and failed to make an impact, and that there is nothing that can be done about it. The truth is that without personal and communal analysis, research, and theological reflection they are swinging away at the air, never connecting with the actual situation nor adjusting their actions to have the greatest impact. They are not clear of their motivations, of their place in the systems they seek to change, or of their complicity in the oppression they seek to overcome. They continue to see things as disconnected and take their experiences at face value.

I remember when it became crystal clear to me that action, "service education," without reflection, without research and

---

[2] Branson and Martinez, *Churches, Cultures and Leadership*, 40.
[3] Branson and Martinez, *Churches, Cultures and Leadership*, 42.

analysis of systems, can do more harm than good. We were serving as a host family for a young woman raised in a conservative Christian household in the suburbs. She was enrolled in a global mission program at the university that required students to immerse themselves in the City of Los Angeles in preparation for a study year abroad. The students were exposed to urban issues such as pluralism, poverty, and oppression, through a variety of immersion experiences. One such exercise required students to spend the night in a homeless shelter. They were to present themselves as homeless, and go through the process of enrolling at a shelter overnight. Though there are some ethical questions raised by this exercise, such as the rightness of privileged young people depriving actual homeless people of beds in order to have a learning experience, the idea was for the students to have a first-hand lived experience of what it is like to be homeless in a big city.

After one night away, the young woman returned home. She had come to the conclusion after one night in the shelter that people in homeless shelters want to be homeless. I asked her what led her to think that, and she said that she had had a conversation with a woman in the shelter who did not want to get a permanent place to live and preferred the freedom afforded her by living on the streets and surviving on supportive services made available to her through organizations such as this shelter. After this conversation, the student was convinced that this must be the case for most homeless people, and that this explained why homelessness was so persistent a problem.

To say I was shocked is an understatement. The conversation that evening consisted of a series of questions I posed to the student: about the woman, her history, the circumstances that brought her to the shelter, her experience seeking permanent housing and work, her mental health status, as well as questions about the bigger issues at play, such as: Why does homelessness happen? How do people become homeless? What kind of services or laws might be necessary to provide adequate housing for people, or to address issues of mental health, addiction, abuse, and violence? By the end of our more intimate conversation, and I am sure after the debriefing with the larger group, the student recognized that her focusing on the individual without analyzing the context, and without asking questions about why things are the way they are, could easily lead to misconceptions. These misconceptions in turn could overemphasize personal responsibility and choice in the face of systemic issues that no one person could overcome or challenge, much less change. Churches in turn might see themselves as powerless to address or impact the systems that cause homelessness and instead seek only to provide relief or respite for the homeless (which is a necessary thing) instead of also acting as agents in history with the power to impact the broader contexts that allow homelessness to happen.

Systemic analysis, theological reflection, and self-awareness that helps to contextualize one's own life experiences are all necessary ingredients in the process of learning how to live and serve people across lines of difference. Leaders especially need to be equipped to envision a different future for themselves, their congregations, and their communities in order to promote and encourage the learning and the change required by the people they serve, both within the congregation and throughout their communities. This learning is most effective when its method reflects the content and the goals of the learning process. The process of education, the methodology, the pedagogy, is seen not only as a vehicle for the transmission of knowledge but as the knowledge that is being transmitted itself. The way one learns is part of what one learns. The traditional banking method of education teaches and embodies the concept that people are empty vessels waiting to be filled by the expert who has all the knowledge. A critical pedagogy, by contrast, assumes that students enter the learning situation with all kinds of knowledge that can be built upon and used in order to increase their knowledge, skills, and ability. The learning begins from the context of the students, builds on their experiences, and problematizes their questions, concerns, and topics for discussion.

Critical Multicultural Education applies this critical/liberative pedagogy to contexts where issues of oppression are multilayered issues of difference. The task of social transformation is more complex and nuanced as the intersection of differences, and the various ways that people and communities experience oppression and privileges are named and explored. Oppression based on race, gender, class, physical abilities, ethnicity, and age does not occur one at a time in people's lives. The intersection of oppression for a poor woman of color, for example, means that the systems that impact her life do so in different ways at different times in different contexts. In a family meeting with her brothers, she may be disempowered because she is female, and her opinion is valued less than the men in her family. At college she may suffer from a lack of access to resources that allow her to take full advantage of the educational opportunity. In a community meeting where most participants are white women, she may be discounted because of the assumptions that her issues are understood and addressed by the other participants, who in actuality have never experienced some of the discrimination she has because of her race, ethnicity, or economic circumstance. Given this particular example, there are also times when this woman has access to certain benefits because she is educated, yet it is only empowering in those contexts which value formal education; she may in a different context—in her community, for example—be marginalized because she is suspected to be out of touch with the challenges faced by those struggling to survive without the benefits schooling can provide.

People's identities, and how these confer privilege or are subject to disenfranchisement, require a multilayered understanding of culture in society. In a multicultural context, such as the United States, valuing and seeking to understand different cultural realities on their own terms requires an intentional act. The assumptions about culture, immigration, and citizenship in our context have often been that people's differences will be assimilated into the dominant culture, or "white America."[4] This assimilation philosophy in its mildest forms leads to an overemphasis on shared culture, without acknowledging the penalties suffered for the differences. In its most extreme forms, it leads to a lack of respect and acceptance of the cultural differences that exist, and the domination that is operative in the social systems and structures that disempower the minority cultures. The response of multicultural educators is to recognize and engage the diversity of cultures in society. But here again, the approaches vary widely, and critical multicultural education argues for an engagement across lines of difference for the purpose of creating a just society. Tolerance, appreciation, and respect are not the end goals. Instead, the goal is a deeper understanding of the ways in which history can be transformed through the forging of alliances across lines of difference, building a movement that benefits from the strengths, gifts, and experiences the various cultures have to offer.

---

[4] Duarte and Smith, *Foundational Perspectives*, 7-8.

Multiculturalism can create allies engaged in social justice. The transformation of the culture in ways that promote democracy, equality, and justice for all people in society is the purpose of such education.[5] This distinction is necessary given neoliberal projects of diversity training in order to exploit the human resources of various cultures and communities towards the end of increased capital production for the upper class. In that context the goal is to maximize productivity by creating a collaborative work environment.[6] Learning about different cultures and how to work well with people across lines of difference allows corporations to access material and human resources internationally. The promotion of tolerance and diversity education in the service of increased labor productivity to maximize profits is not the goal of critical multicultural education.[7]

Instead of seeking to domesticate difference in order to avoid conflict, critical multicultural education seeks to problematize, question, and disrupt the status quo. The questioning of societal assumptions, especially regarding corporate and mass-produced culture is essential for analyzing the context and the systems that sustain inequality, unemployment, and oppressive hierarchical systems necessary to the operation of unbridled capitalism. An analysis of the systems of oppression operative in society, those that oppress and disenfranchise persons and communities on the basis of differences in gender identity/sexuality, race, class, and physical and mental abilities is necessary to an understanding of how each person is engaged and implicated in the system and in order to assess and explore ways of resisting complicity and compliance.

Church leaders in particular lead organizations that have as their mission the liberation and flourishing of peoples. Their mission

---

[5] "At its inception, multicultural education challenged power relations, particularly racism. However, over time, power has often become displaced by more comfortable concepts such as tolerance, which has led to apolitical versions of multicultural education." Sleeter and Grant, *Making Choices for Multicultural Education*, 184.

[6] Claudia Matus and Marta Infante, "Undoing Diversity; Knowledge and Neoliberal Discourses in Colleges of Education," *Discourse: Studies in the Cultural Politics of Education*, 33 (2011): 300-301.

[7] This reflects an alternative, conflictive, purpose of education. The purposing of education for purely capitalistic economic advantage can be seen in the study: "A Nation at Risk (National Commission on Excellence in Education, 1983), quoted in Sleeter and Grant, *Making Choices for Multicultural Education*, 18.

to participate in God's work of liberation and reconciliation can be informed by this process of critical reflection and systemic analysis. It is a way to understand and take seriously the work at hand, as described in Ephesians.

> For our struggle is not against enemies of blood and flesh, but against the rulers, against the authorities, against the cosmic powers of this present darkness, against the spiritual forces of evil in the heavenly places. (Eph. 6:12, NRSV)

That is to say that we need to understand that things as they seem on the surface are not all that is going on, that what influences and governs peoples' lives and circumstances is spiritual in nature (greed, envy, hatred, fear, violence) and also thoroughly embodied in systems and structures of oppression, ideologies of domination, and currencies of violence. Bringing forth an alternative society in which these social realities are challenged and dismantled is the mission of the church, first through the example of the ordering of its own communal life and then through its ministry of healing and transformation in the world. A church that welcomes and seeks to serve and be transformed by the marginalized is creating a culture; it provides leadership through its very existence. It becomes a case that argues for the possibilities of alternative practices that transform people and communities.

In Latin America this understanding of the purpose and mission of the church is described as Integral Mission. It is rooted in an expanded understanding of the character and scope of evangelism. The contributors to *The Local Church, Agent of Transformation: An Ecclesiology for Integral Mission* offer a theology of Integral Mission, reflecting on its biblical, theological and ecclesial understandings, and the implications for the work and identity of the Church.[8] Especially useful is the theological framework offered by Nancy E. Bedford, who understands integral mission as a re-appropriation of the Trinitarian understanding of the great commission as presented in the Gospel of John.[9] Rooting the church firmly in its belief in a Triune God allows for the re-integration of

---

[8] Tetsunao Yamamori and C. Rene Padilla, eds., *The Local Church, Agent of Transformation: An Ecclesiology for Integral Mission* (Buenos Aires: Kairos, 2004).
[9] Nancy E. Bedford, "The Theology of Integral Mission and Community Discernment," in *The Local Church*, ed. Yamamori and Padilla, 99-103.

the incarnational nature of church and the central role for the Spirit (and by extension the feminine) in the discernment and vocation of the church as community and of God's people as empowered ministers.

The incarnation is a challenge to the church to engage the cultural realities of the context in which they are called to do ministry. In the early church the integration of the Gentiles became a decisive moment in the understanding of what it means to be Christian. It was decided that converts did not have to take on the cultural aspects that embodied the Gospel. Instead the Gospel was to be offered to and by the cultural context, and Bedford offers guidelines, drawn from the Church's theological tradition, for this contextualization that preserves the integrity of the Gospel message, keeping it free from idolatry and committed to "the poor, marginalized and socially excluded."[10] Latin American cultures, with their characteristic hybridity is the locus of the incarnation and the ministries offered, they bring the transforming work of the Spirit, the Good News, to all aspects of human life, indeed to all of creation. This holistic approach is the heart of Integral Mission, and it provides for the possibility of overcoming the "absurd polarization" of the social gospel and the gospel of the Word.[11]

The Church therefore is called into social/vocational discernment about the who, how, where and when of ministry as it seeks to serve Christ in the poor, the widowed, the marginalized and the outcast. This discernment can be structured utilizing the classic tradition of "*lectio, meditatio, oratio* and *tentatio*," a hermeneutical reflective circle that leads to a Trinitarian engagement in mission.[12] Engaging scripture (*lectio*) in spiritual reflection (*meditatio*) on what questions it brings to the context and what questions the context brings to it, moves the community to prayerfully (*oratio*) engage and act (*tentatio*) in ways that respond to the call of God to embody and live out the Gospel message in transformative service to and with others. This ongoing process of discernment, engages critically the realities of the social/cultural context and acts to participate in the Spirit's transformation and renewal of all Creation, including the social structures that do not promote full life and liberation for the

---

[10] Bedford, "Theology of Integral Mission," 103.
[11] Bedford, "Theology of Integral Mission," 105.
[12] Bedford, "Theology of Integral Mission," 115.

children of God. This theological cycle of action-reflection, which utilizes the ancient Christian practices, is offered as a process of disciple formation.[13]

Bedford's model roots the critical formation process in the theological and spiritual understandings of the Christian tradition. It both grounds and informs the work of formation of all believers, but especially of those called to lead congregations that seek to be responsive to the lived social and cultural realities of the ministerial contexts, their parishes. As with the methodology offered by Branson and Martinez, the engagement of communal reading of scripture, prayer, and a study and analysis of both the history of the traditions of the church and the context of ministry, anchors and informs the application of critical pedagogies in the formation of church leaders. The faith tradition, in this case Christianity, and the denominational and congregational institutions become central cultural features to both analyze and inform the processes of critical multicultural education and leadership formation. They offer another multicultural reality that further complicates and nuances the approaches and strategies of engagement both with the church and the communities in which they live and minister.

In critical multicultural education, culture is broadly defined as people's practices, histories, art, and ways of viewing the world. As such, culture includes:

- Ethnic cultures, identified by their roots in particular nation states, some of which are deemed inferior in comparison to the superior, normative, cultural standard of western European culture.
- Racial groupings, socially constructed and utilized in colonial projects of domination and exploitation, and maintained in neocolonial and postcolonial contexts as hierarchies of privilege and oppression.
- Gender identity and sexuality, where heteronormativity is privileged, and nonconformity is punished through legal reprisal, social persecution, and disenfranchisement of human and civil rights.
- Class and caste stratifications, which devalue persons who are not of the powerful, affluent elite, and whose work and

---

[13] Bedford, "Theology of Integral Mission," 121.

livelihood is subjugated to fulfill the needs of the owners of capital and means of production.

- Physical and mental abilities, where communities who function in the world in a way that is alternative because their mental faculties or their sensory or physical capacities are not physiotypical and therefore not taken into consideration in planning and development, creating an inaccessible society.

The term 'critical multicultural education,' and 'multiculturalism' in general, arises as a response to the hegemony of European-based educational institutions that only recognize white, western, male, heterosexual, physiotypical, upper-class history, activity, and culture as worthy of being taught and learned. Those who historically have been dominated and oppressed do not find their histories, perspectives, and realities included in the educational canon. Only one perspective and epistemology is privileged and there is a great deal of resistance to the inclusion of perspectives of "the other." The inclusion of oppressed people's history is seen as an infringement on the privilege enjoyed by the dominant group to define the national/historical narrative. In the 1960s the critique of these types of educational assumptions brought the history of oppressed minorities/subjugated populations into the academy and other learning contexts. It was this movement that sought to hear the voices of the marginalized by including them in the corpus of knowledge being taught in public schools and institutions of higher learning. This movement led not only to the inclusion of other stories but the questioning of the frameworks and conclusions that were assumed as the only way to analyze and understand what was going on. This questioning and critique problematized the prevalent understanding of history, culture, arts, beauty, etc. It asked: What perspective is being presented? Who benefits from this narrative? Who is disenfranchised by it? What are the other perspectives present in the contexts that are not being voiced or represented?

Critical multicultural education distinguishes itself from other approaches to engage diversity in its resistance to assimilationism, which despite the nomenclature seeks to emphasize cultural sameness rather than cultural diversity.[14] Duarte and Smith define

---

[14] Duarte and Smith, *Foundational Perspectives*, 5.

multiculturalism as sharing a critical stance towards assimilation and an oppositional stance towards the dominant social order, but these stances, based on philosophical perspectives, can vary widely with regards to the strategies employed to achieve a just, democratic and inclusive society.[15] In their designation of perspectives critical multiculturalism is one of four perspectives (ethnic studies, antiracist, and liberal democratic being the other three) that stands in the critical theory tradition, in addition to combining a wide variety of theoretical traditions.[16] This approach incorporates liberative praxis, anti-racist theory and action, and seeks to practice radical democracy in the classroom, politicizing the space so as to undermine domesticating ideologies and practices. It also includes in its analytic tool kit negative dialectics and poststructuralist critiques, which discourage a too quick assumption that dialogue is sufficient to the task of just engagement and inclusion, and that unity across lines of difference can quickly become unity at the expense of difference.[17] This is further informed by a *borderlands* or *mestizo* consciousness, so that

> From a macro point of view, the multicultural borderland defines cultural experience as the crisscrossing of the lives of diverse people(s) and expresses an understanding of self and society as processual, dynamic, open ended, or *mestizo*.[18]

As critical multicultural pedagogy identifies and teaches about the oppressive systems that are operative in society, the work of liberation becomes a shared project. As people study and claim their own identity, the separate silos sometimes created by identity politics are challenged and dismantled. People can recognize the multifaceted nature of their identity. The intersection and overlapping of identities and their relative power and privilege (depending on the context) can be acknowledged. In some contexts, a person is privileged, in others that same person is disenfranchised. This reality provides a bridge between communities, and even a

---

[15] Duarte and Smith, *Foundational Perspectives*, 9. The goal of their anthology is to present the various perspectives of multiculturalism so that depending on context and situation, educators can comfortably vary their approaches and strategies as appropriate, and develop "their own brand of multicultural education."
[16] Duarte and Smith, *Foundational Perspectives*, 18.
[17] Duarte and Smith, *Foundational Perspectives*, 19-20.
[18] Duarte and Smith, *Foundational Perspectives*, 20.

point of departure for the liberation of the oppressor. Freire contended that the project of liberation is not only for those who are disenfranchised in society. The oppressor must also be humanized, for the liberation of all humanity is the purpose of the project.[19] Alliances based on a commonality of purpose and a compassion borne of one's understanding of the intersectionality of identities and oppressions organizes communities for power that can be brought to bear on deconstructing oppressive systems and social structures and constructing a just democratic society.

This reality and the necessity of a broader understanding of culture and how it is operative in and among communities brings to the fore that although at times groups of people may choose to operate out of a common or shared culture, most contexts and communities are multicultural, and assumptions must be named and tested in order to respect the dignity of the people present. This is common in churches, where the shared denominational identity and the shared practices create a common culture. Without intentional engagement of different styles of worship, different spiritual experiences and needs, and different ways to organize the work, too often the shared culture is simply by default the historically dominant culture. The ability to recognize and challenge the assumptions present in the shared culture allows new and alternative expressions of communal life to surface. It renews the practice, deepens the exploration for the community and for the members individually.

It is this process of continual exploration and questioning that must be "institutionalized," or normalized. The challenge of creating and sustaining a "learning organization"[20] is to make it the norm to ask questions, seek a variety of perspectives, and listen to the different experiences in the room rather than continue to do things the "way we have always done things." This will respond to the natural frustration of having to deconstruct (cultural) assumptions at every turn. Making action-reflection the accepted learning modality and incorporating this process into every area of corporate church life — liturgy, scripture study, prayer, service, activism, formation, committee work, leadership board meetings,

---

[19] Freire, *Pedagogy of the Oppressed: 30th Anniversary Edition*, 44.
[20] Peter Senge, *The Fifth Discipline: The Art and Practice of the Learning Organization* (New York: Doubleday/Currency, 1990).

etc. — is to embrace critical multiculturalism and its requisite power sharing. This practice can become an embodiment of the spiritual belief that God is directing our lives, pausing to be curious about what God is doing in our midst, what new thing God is about to reveal. "Behold I make all things new," (Rev. 21:5 NKJV) becomes the mantra of an organization that engages in continual growth and development. Each of these cases reflects both the benefit of engaging critically issues of oppression and difference and the weakness of an approach that either seeks to "move past" these issues or live as if they have been sufficiently dealt with once they have been engaged. The curiosity and the exploration must be ongoing in order to impact the culture of the community, and to continually encourage the growth of the leaders, and their ongoing engagement in the creation of a just and life giving community.

Lay Leadership Development at St. Mary's Church

The most significant formative event in the life of the church of St. Mary's was the experience of internment during World War II. The period of ministry prior to internment consisted for most (Japanese) parishioners of learning how to live and thrive in a new country with different expectations and cultural assumptions. The exact nature of this process is not documented in detail, but there were classes such as English language classes, Preschool classes and Sunday School classes that taught in direct and indirect ways the norms and expectations of the new society and culture. There was a network of support, through which employment and housing were secured. There were social activities, which provided respite from the work of assimilation, and allowed members to fellowship with others who shared their language, experience, and culture. The clergy modeled how to respond in the face of persecution and social injustice. Their response emphasized respect for authority, dignity in the face of adversity, loyalty, and trust in church leadership. There were other voices, other leaders that made different choices.[21] The parish priests, both father and son, may have longed for more vocal condemnation of government policies by the church on behalf of Japanese Episcopalians in particular, and the internment policy

---

[21] Daisuke Kitagawa's "Open Letter to Fellow Christians in the USA," criticized the internment and lamented the effects it would have on future generations. See Gillespie, "Japanese-American Episcopalians," 5.

in general, but they would not challenge the leadership or the policy publicly. The combination of civic and social disenfranchisement and the cultural values of loyalty, conformity and non-conflictual behavior seem to have left them few options. Given the times, a different reaction would have produced the same result.[22]

The Episcopal Church sought to support their Japanese members by requesting that those in San Francisco and Los Angeles be interned together for mutual support, maintain a separate worship service and, by creating a fund, to purchase their properties for later return. The permission to maintain their religious practices intact, and to be interned with their clergy leadership allowed a continuity of practice as a community. The Episcopal women's auxiliaries provided them with worship materials that allowed them to create a traditional worship space within the confines of the accommodations available. The communities eventually settled into a rhythm of life, organized by the leadership of their clergy; they stayed informed about the community at the other camp, and shared joys and sorrow throughout their interment.[23] It cemented the community, its values, its perspective, not only for the Issei, and Nisei generation but by extension for the Sansei[24] generation as well. The bicultural acclimation that had begun for the Nisei generation was interrupted and supplanted with this shared multigenerational experience that was distinct from the rest of American society. The silence that they brought to the camp continued when they left, and years later they still could not find their voice to talk about the experience.[25]

Awareness of the hegemony of whiteness was not absent in this community. The reality defined their lives in the States, and the lesson learned and transmitted was that they needed to acquiesce to that hegemony. Sympathizers emphasized the importance of integration, identifying the ghettoization of the churches and the communities as contributing to the internment.[26] The lesson learned was that integration and loss of distinctive ("alienating") cultural

---

[22] Gillespie, "Japanese-American Episcopalians," 5.
[23] Gillespie, "Japanese-American Episcopalians," 12.
[24] These terms are used in the context of the United States to designate the immigrant generation, the children of those immigrants, and the grandchildren of the immigrants, corresponding to the Japanese words for the numbers 1,2, and 3.
[25] Gillespie, "Japanese-American Episcopalians," 5.
[26] Gillespie, "Japanese-American Episcopalians," 10.

practices was the way to live in American society. The work of the parish was to integrate, to join in with white Americans in worship, professional, and civic life.

All of these hard learned lessons of survival mitigate against a desire to question and challenge social structures. As American cultural norms shift and make it more socially acceptable to articulate perspectives that encourage and support civil rights for minorities and marginalized persons, these shifts have also become a part of the life of St. Mary's. The introduction of women in clerical leadership, and changes in worship, were controversial, resisted, but eventually accepted.[27]

Involvement in the wider life of the church, and engagement with community groups that would sustain the long-time activities of the church (youth, preschool, gardens) were ways the wider community was engaged. This engagement was primarily through community social services. Participation in these services and educational programs was the medium for community involvement with the church. Actual participation in the life of the church, defined here, as interaction with church members, was limited; as a commuter church most members were on church grounds only on Sundays, while "outreach" programs occurred during the week.

The lay leader training did not challenge this level of interaction. The trainings and materials were those designed for "traditional" suburban churches in the Episcopal Church, which is exactly the identity with which the majority of the membership identified. Their ministries were the social service programs offered, where they helped the community. Nothing in the material or discussion invited them into a partnership with their neighbors to transform their community. The broader involvements that are celebrated by the congregation are those in which they participate in the work of the broader institutional life of the church, not those that address social change, or engagement with issues of justice and oppression. Although some members may have been involved in these activities, they are not reflected in the parish profile, as descriptive of the church's wider involvement. For example, although Alix Evans, the previous rector, was known for her work to abolish the death penalty, a cause for which she provided leadership

---

[27] "St. Mary's Parish Profile, 2001."

throughout the diocese, this is not listed as place of diocesan involvement and leadership in the parish profile.[28]

The process initiated by the parish survey, in which members were asked about their vision for the future of the parish, provided the opportunity for learning and problem solving. It became the first step in a leadership development process that invited members into the pastoral circle of action-reflection. There was a problem for which there were no easy answers: What *is* the vision of this parish for the future? What should be our goals? The questions led to action: getting more information, a deeper engagement in the context, which in turn provided more material for reflection and further action. The values and needs of the Japanese American membership differed widely from that of the local community (as represented by the members of the Spanish worship service) but were not in conflict with it. The reflection provided in the sermon about the past of the church presented the heritage and history as a source of vision for the future. It connected the story of the parish to the larger gospel story, and allowed the church to re-envision and reengage its mission. Father Van Horn served as the facilitator (educator), problematizing the way they understood themselves: who, what, and why are they church? In contrast to naming yet again the need to change and welcome others, they chose to act. The reflection on the sermon, the engagement of the questions and the decision to act, by reaching out to others in the congregation to learn about the church system in a different way, was actual movement for transformative ministry.

Small groups were created to explore further the social and institutional systems that they sought to impact. The groups were able to bring back the reflections of the whole community on its past and its role in the present, the needs to be addressed, and the ability of people to participate in a new phase of their church life together. They came up with the idea for a Mission Recovery Project, a People's Energy Audit, and a Local Community Needs Audit. This engaged the whole congregation in reflection. Through this process they: shared their fears of losing their heritage and their willingness to move forward, inventoried their resources, how many hours each person could dedicate to ministry in the church, and identified

---

[28] "St. Mary's Parish Profile, 2010," 8.

possible ministries, and ways they could address the needs of the community.

The second sermon by Father Van Horn provided an opportunity for further reflection on what they had learned and how that might inform their vision of their future mission and the qualities they would need in their future rector. The community was vitalized by this new vision; they decided they would dedicate themselves to minister to the needs of the immigrants in their community, continuing the call they had lived into at their founding, specifically of serving the needs of the Japanese immigrants.

The current vestry, under the leadership of the new rector, continues to engage this pastoral action-reflection circle during the vestry development time at the beginning of each vestry meeting. It is ongoing reflection that leads to action and further reflection on how to live into the vision of being a church that ministers to immigrant families, regardless of origin. They have reflected on possible partners with whom they can collaborate in addressing the needs of the immigrant community that surrounds their parish. They have identified the leaders of various organizations comprised by and for immigrants, finding partners *with* whom to do ministry instead of people *for* whom to do ministry.

This partnering and collaboration has led to deeper engagement with their neighbors. It has meant welcoming the neighborhood into the church. They are using the building as a community base for community programs and activities; it is where the community works and serves, not simply a place where it comes to receive services and go on its way. It has become the site for cultural celebrations that are integrated into the church's calendar of activities and celebrations. In order to do this space was opened up. Spaces that had been taken up with storing the relics of past activities became sites for new activities. The community groups have a place to meet, store their materials, and plan and execute their activities. The Oaxacan community, over time, has gone from simply using space for their music classes and festive gatherings to having the statue of the patron saint of their village in Mexico, San Cristobal (St. Christopher), housed in the sanctuary. The prayer rituals and acts of devotion of this community are now a part of daily life at St. Mary's. It has become their place of worship, and so their traditions are being woven into the traditions of St. Mary's as seen in the Christmas Festival.

The Oaxacan leadership, along with the staff of the parish, the neighbors involved in the community gardens, and other neighbors became involved in the opening of a new park in the community. The design of the park would have rendered yet another public space inaccessible to the majority of the community.[29] Upon hearing that a park was being designed near the church, the church staff attending planning meetings, where they saw that the plans would annex public land, heavily trafficked, and put a gate around it for use by members of the Korean community to hold cultural events and activities. The denial of access to the majority of the community for a park on public lands, in part using public funds for its development, seemed unjust to the leaders of St. Mary's, and they discussed the issue with their network. As a result of that discussion, they decided to reach out to the Koreatown Immigrant Workers Association (KIWA).[30] Together this group of concerned neighbors strategized, researched, and went and testified before the City Council committee, which led to a fuller participation in the planning committee, and a change in the architectural plans for the park. Other members of the committee that had been uncomfortable with the original plan aligned themselves with this "St. Mary's coalition," and supported the new, much more open plan for a park that could be enjoyed by all of the members of the community, and not only the business leaders that saw this as a show piece, rather than as a neighborhood park. This quality of life issue impacted all the diverse sectors in the community. Engaging it meant orientation to the city government system, introduction to the stakeholders, and the powerful leaders of the community, as well as shared analysis about how to be most strategic to challenge the plan without causing a rift between different constituencies in the community. This action

---

[29] A block away from the church there is a small park with benches and a Korean-style gazebo, which, although purportedly a community park, is gated and locked, making it inaccessible to the community. This new project was on track to annex and close yet more public space, for very restricted use.

[30] Koreatown Immigrant Workers Alliance: "The mission of KIWA is to build the power of immigrant workers and residents and to organize a progressive grassroots leadership to transform our workplaces and communities, in Koreatown and beyond." KIWA website accessed January 20, 2015, http://kiwa.org/.

successfully empowered the members of the community, and led to a shared success among different groups in the neighborhood that did not usually work together.[31]

The case of St. Mary's Episcopal Church offers an example of liberative pedagogy facilitating change by creating the space for generative themes to surface. The church problematized the need for a future direction, inviting reflection on how the experience of parishioners and the analysis of the context could inform the future direction of the church. The action taken by the vestry, to invite the congregation into this same type of reflection, where opinions were not simply solicited but where the congregation also, through the Mission Recovery Project, was presented with questions that challenged the assumptions of what it meant to honor their legacy and build on their heritage, became another opportunity for leadership development through a liberative pedagogy. The ability to recognize that the need to respond to the current context had become critical was, I believe, facilitated by the invitation to look at the history of the church in a different way. To preserve the heritage of St. Mary's was not to seek and serve Japanese Americans in a context in which the dominant cultural groups are Latinos/Latinas and Koreans, but to seek and serve immigrants seeking a better life for their children, learning about and engaging a different culture, bringing their cultural contributions into a new context.

This reflection led the congregation's leadership once again to explore their context, their community, this time with a goal of identifying other organizations engaged in the work of serving immigrants and improving community life. The shift from providing services to the disenfranchised to seeking to work with others to change the situation that was causing the disenfranchisement can be seen in the coming together of various neighbors, already in some relationship to the parish, to address the designs of the area park under development. The action of researching the project, identifying the stakeholders and the power players, and seeking allies that represented the breadth of the community's diversity created a wider circle of reflection. The church provided leadership for the opposition to a development that would have further disenfranchised the community members.

---

[31] Conversation with the Rev. Anna Olson, current rector of St. Mary's Church, September 1, 2014.

It also provided an opportunity for the community members, some highly organized (the Oaxacan community) and others more loosely affiliated (the families from the community gardens), to learn about civic government: the role and power of local planning committees, the engagement of Los Angeles City Council representatives, and testifying in hearings before City Council Committees. It brought these groups into working relationship with KIWA, a non-profit organizing group engaged in bettering the lives of the immigrant workers in their neighborhood, creating a concrete link for the parish between its new understanding of its mission to the local community and organizational partners that reflected that community. Networking with KIWA, who organizes workers of Korean and Latino descent, is an expansion of its partnerships beyond its usual collaborative partner, the Little Tokyo Service Center, identified with the people of Japanese descent, and not located in St. Mary's Koreatown neighborhood.

As the congregation continues to explore ways to live into its new vision and understanding of mission, intentional exploration of issues impacting their community and their role as agents of transformation in that context must be integrated into the life of the congregation. Christian formation for the congregation should include opportunities to explore the faith story of hope and transformation as it engages the world it is called to serve. The community needs assessment that was conducted as part of the rector's search process identified the top four needs of the community as employment/jobs, housing, day care and immigration/citizenship classes. Using these themes in planning bible studies, retreats, service projects, and other formation practices, could provide the congregation with continued opportunities to reflect on their experience and their context, research and learn about the possibilities for action, and to take action and then reflect on what they have learned, on how it informs their faith, on what God might be calling them to do in this context, and on how they are being called to minister and to be change agents. The exploration of these issues and especially their causes will provide opportunities to identify oppressive systems at play in their context. How are racism, classism, gender and sexual orientation discrimination, issues of physical and mental illness and disability or access, ageism, ethnic biases, operative in the system as it exists? What does the Christian tradition say about this, what do they know from their own experience? How might they as a congregation be equipped and called to impact these systems to make them more just, and in that way improve the quality of life of the community of which they are a part and which they are called to serve? Raising and exploring these questions through the congregation's faith practices, in sermons, at vestry meetings, through quiet days, on retreat, through programs and activities with children and youth, would integrate a multicultural pedagogy into the formation opportunities provided by the church. It would engage the tradition's formation tools and spiritual practices (Scripture, prayer, exhortation, teaching, fasting, testifying/witnessing, and study) in a critical way that takes seriously the historic context for the revelation of God. The theology of the incarnation calls for engaging a God who engages history, and as followers and disciples of this God incarnate in Jesus Christ, the church is called to do the same. Engaging the context critically with an eye to transformation is the call of the church; the methodology and approach offered by multicultural critical educations equip the church to live out this call faithfully.

Lay Leadership Development at Holy Faith Church

Holy Faith Episcopal Church has had more structured opportunities for intentional leadership development woven into the fabric of the life of the church than St. Mary's Church. The racial, ethnic and class composition of the church slowly shifted to reflect the changing demographics of the city. First African American, then Latino and African immigrants were welcomed into the church and as these diverse communities were integrated into the life of the parish issues of race, gender and sexual orientation were addressed head on. Workshops and dialogue opportunities were offered to the membership, and many leaders participated in these conversations. The dialogue process began with people sharing their personal stories about the issues being discussed, their experiences and their understandings. This meant an embodiment of the issues: these were no longer social issues at the center of culture wars out somewhere in the public square, but instead the realities of the lives of their fellow church members. Sensitivity and care were called to the fore in a conversation that could have easily degenerated into conflicts over interpretation of Scripture, or the changes (good and bad) of the practices of the church. Instead, the opportunity to dialogue across lines of difference led to a stronger identity as a diverse parish, and to members valuing the differences among them as a gift to the local and wider church. This was reflected in the shared celebrations of each other's cultures. The church calendar reflected the diversity of the congregation in special events celebrated annually: Black History Month, Holy Faith Day, African Sunday, and Las Posadas. There was also a strong, committed group of activists who worked together as the Outreach Commission and later as the Justice and Mercy committee (JAMS). This group engaged issues of race, gender, poverty, and economic inequality through their presentations in the parish and throughout the diocese and also through direct action, working with the local unions on issues of living wage and freedom to organize for better work conditions. The afterschool program, the Alternatives to Violence and the health programming of the congregation were also seen as direct responses to issues affecting their local community. Youth violence and health disparities were being addressed by providing a safe space for children and youth, and health and nutrition programming for all ages.

This model, however, had limitations that might have been better addressed with a pedagogy that assumes ongoing learning through a process of action-reflection. Discussions and workshops were held, but not all members of the church participated. Preaching provided ongoing opportunities for reflection, but except for a smaller group within the parish (Outreach/JAMS committees) the majority of the congregation did not undertake action. Some of the activities sponsored by the Outreach Commission, especially around issues of hunger, such as writing to lawmakers to advocate for programs that addressed poverty, required minimal engagement. People saw the workshops and dialogues as having dealt with the issue once and for all, whereas in reality the magnitude of the issues and the pernicious and insidious nature of oppression in society called for ongoing opportunities to engage in reflection that could lead to action. People who were new to the congregation, or who had left for a period of time and returned, did not have the opportunity to engage in this formative process, and their development as leaders was limited because of it.

The need for ongoing action-reflection, and engagement of issues of oppression can be seen in the reaction of many of the church members to the election of Gene V. Robinson as Bishop of New Hampshire. In response to the affirmation of the election by the General Convention, a large group of church members left. Some left to join more conservative Christian churches, others to form their own break-away churches within the "Anglican tradition," but each left stating that they could not in good conscience continue to be part of a church that had acted in such an untraditional manner. Although there had been discussions about issues of sexuality and sexual orientation, and the congregation understood that all were welcome in God's house, as articulated in their statement of welcome, this proved to be a statement of tolerance, rather than a commitment to the equality of all persons. In a congregation embodying as much diversity as Holy Faith does in terms of race, class, ethnicity, gender, sexual orientation, theological, physical and mentally a-typicality, the ability to come to agreement that the church should embrace everyone regardless of their differences is significant. Yet one wonders whether ongoing conversations about the definition and place of church tradition and interpretations of Scripture, especially as these were understood in the face of social issues, might not have provided more strength to their commitment to inclusion, and more resilience in the face of the stormy changes facing the church.

The visioning work engaged in later, that invited a study of the context and an exploration of the experiences of people in the congregation with issues that were impacting the congregation, was a re-visiting of this process. Yet again it missed the opportunity of leading to ongoing formation activities that would bring to the fore the call of the church in its internal and external life as an institution in the business of addressing, and to the degree possible, eradicating oppressive systems and their impact on the community. The dialogue sermons, in which members broke into small groups and discussed the application of the scripture and the brief reflection provided by the rector, were one place where ongoing formation occurred. But these did not happen consistently and were interrupted when time and energy were redirected to address other parish issues. The importance of leadership holding up not only the vision of the parish, but the history of the parish in living into a transformative future, became apparent when a long-time member elected to leadership was surprised to hear that dialogues and workshops on issues of oppression had been conducted in the church. They had occurred during a gap in her attendance, and she had not had the opportunity to engage in this leadership development process. Some formation occurred as part of the vestry reflection discussions at the beginning of meetings, and the exploration of policy decisions, such as taking a public stance against the death penalty or in support of car wash workers organizing for better work conditions and living wages. Yet these conversations inevitably pointed to the need for ongoing formation of the whole congregation on the implications of Scripture and tradition in the face of issues of justice and oppression in current society.

Vestry orientations at Holy Faith Church tended to be technical in nature, informing new and ongoing members of their administrative responsibilities, and not encouraging an understanding of leadership that emphasized articulating the vision of the parish and identifying new leaders and providing opportunities for the formation of those new leaders. The activism of the parish was still primarily in the hands of the clergy and a small group of church members. Seeing it not as one among many activities of the church, but as central to the identity and mission of the church, would have meant strategizing to find ways to incorporate more members and especially all the leaders, in the work of social justice and social transformation, albeit through a variety of means. Not all were called to be activists, but all were called to reflect on how their faith put to action challenged social assumptions that maintained systemic oppression. In order to strengthen leadership development for the changes and challenges of urban, pluralistic society, these learning opportunities need to be woven into the ongoing programming of the church, through opportunities to question, analyze, act, and reflect.

Implications for Leadership Development presented by the Cases of St. Mary's and Holy Faith Church

Each of these cases presents a congregation that sought to respond to the multicultural reality of its community, both within the congregation and in its surrounding community, its neighborhood context. In both cases the congregational leadership development included training on technical and administrative responsibilities that sustain the church institutionally, issues of administration and viability being part of the work of any organization's leadership. In both cases, the congregations were confronted with challenges that had their origin in oppressive systems operative in the wider culture. For St. Mary's Church, this is most dramatically encapsulated in their experience of interment during World War II. There the hegemony of whiteness led to an unjust loss of property and freedom. For Holy Faith Church, the process of integration, first of African Americans and later of Latinas(os) and African immigrants, into a white, English-speaking, primarily middle-class congregation, was what brought them into dialogue on issues of racism, economic injustice, ethnic prejudice, gender issues, and other forms of social oppression. In each case formation and leadership development sought to address these issues. In the case of St. Mary's Church, the congregation sought to integrate into the larger society and its dominant culture. The cost of maintaining a distinct culture, while seeking to adapt and adopt a new one, had been too high. The goal was to prove that their distinctiveness did not make them a threat, and that they sought to be productive, law-abiding citizens of the United States. In the case of Holy Faith, some adaptation was also at play, as many new members integrated into the congregation shared the class values, and some immigrants also shared the class assumptions, of the dominant, middle-class culture of the denomination. Training leadership to live in diverse community entails engaging the diversity head on and discussing and learning about the impact social oppression had on the members of the community. For many members, it also meant working to change those structures because of their faith.

Both congregations have also come to utilize a liberative pedagogy as they develop strategies to continue to find ways to be responsive to their diverse context. They have explored their communities, and through conversation with members who represent the cultures that surround their churches, they have identified the needs of the community and found partners in the work of improving the quality of life in their communities by addressing the oppressive systems that negatively impact the community. Through reflection and action, investigation, and analysis they have participated with their neighbors in actions that have improved the lives of local residents and have partnered with other community-based agencies, allowing them to leverage more power through these alliances.

In each case, however, the integration of a critical multicultural pedagogy has been difficult to sustain. Although issues of oppression are explored, and dialogue and reflection have led to action, the ability to make them a part of the ongoing formation of members and leaders has not been formalized. Institutionalizing the values, goals, and strategies of this pedagogy will require a regular practice of study, reflection, prayer, and action as part of the church's Christian formation. It will also require that the problematizing of issues be a practice that takes place in different settings, so that every aspect of church life and mission incorporates this practice, and the learning that it ignites.

Therefore, in addition to the ongoing formation that is done intentionally through formation programs and activities as well as sermons, there is a need to establish a norm that certain questions will be present in every conversation and decision taken on by the church. These questions should seek to problematize the discussion, to tease out the complexities. The formation of these questions can be the result of dialogue about a set of issues, and actions taken in response. These questions in turn can themselves be presented for reflection and analysis in other settings. For example, if the Altar Guild is struggling with incorporating new members, they might ask questions that identify the current culture and practice employed, how it facilitates and/or is an obstacle to the incorporation of new members, and what systemic changes can be incorporated to welcome newcomers. For example, the meeting schedule can be changed, and the training can happen one-on-one to incorporate new members whose work schedule will not permit them to participate in the daytime or weekend meetings that have been the norm in the past. Asking certain questions will serve the purpose of questioning the status quo, of disrupting assumptions that sustain oppressive or exclusive systems and practices and can form a type of practice for empowerment and alliance building in themselves. Some such questions that suggest themselves in the face of a diverse community are:

Who is not present in this conversation? What can be done to facilitate their participation in the discussion? This might help to uncover issues of access, such as transportation to and from events, childcare for families with younger children, programming possibilities for young people and children, so that events are intentionally multi-generational, and translation for those who are monolingual but interested in being in dialogue with people who speak a different language.

How will spiritual practices be engaged so that the community is grounding its common life on practices beyond worship on Sunday mornings? Strategies for praying and studying together can take into account the challenges presented by distance and time constraints. Prayer and study group members could stay in conversation and accountable for commitments via email or social media or telephone calls. The whole congregation could read a book on theology or scripture together that explores the topics of justice, inclusion, healing, and transformation creating a shared study, and providing some content for conversations during the social hour.

What would be the ideal circumstance given the values of the Gospel? What are the obstacles to this ideal? What actions do these obstacles suggest we might consider undertaking? This could uncover the complex issues that sustain hunger, unemployment, and homelessness in a community. It might raise suggestions about changes in policy and procedure within the church that limit the participation of the community or inhibit the potential leadership of newer members of the congregation. It might invite deeper study into the causes of economic destabilization in urban communities or ways to improve the access to the buildings.

How can we learn more about each other and the differences reflected in our communities? This might lead to a commitment to read literature written by people from different communities within the U.S. or from other countries represented (or not) in the congregation. It might suggest social activities that can expose members to a different worldview, planning a movie night, watching movies by artists of color or independent films that are not easily accessible to most church members. It might encourage reaching out to other worshipping congregations in the community, especially those of different faith traditions. It might include participation in a community festival hosted by a local mosque, synagogue, or temple.

Creating a learning organization where questions are welcome and a regular part of the way people are with each other, in different settings, situations, and circumstances, would support a culture where on-going learning is occurring on issues of oppression, liberation, and transformation.

In both these cases, at Holy Faith Church and at St. Mary's Church, the clergy play the primary role of facilitators, providing the opportunities for reflection, a deeper exploration of Scripture and leading discussions that problematized the congregations' understanding of the context and the possible responses to issues limiting the life possibilities of those involved. This suggests that as the primary educators of the congregation, the clergy also need to embrace this role of facilitator/agitator. In these cases, clergy took on that role, and identified key questions that led to substantive discussions that then supported action and changes within the congregation and in their wider communities. However, traditionally clergy are not formed in their educational processes to serve in this role. Similar to the training of schoolteachers, the training of clergy does not emphasize problematizing. On the contrary, clergy are trained to comfort people in the face of unjust and difficult situations, and to provide technical fixes to systemic problems. Rarely are they trained to analyze the systems and seek radical transformation of unjust policies and procedures. Churches are accustomed to being institutions that stabilize society, instead of ones that seek to transform society. The role that the clergy of St. Mary's took on during World War II was not uncommon, as can be seen from the response of other church leaders at the time; clergy were not expected, nor encouraged, to challenge openly unjust government policy. Instead, the church sought to make the best of a bad situation. In this way churches, like schools, uphold the status quo.

In order for clergy to be empowered and encouraged to take risks in questioning social constructions whether they be of race, or gender identities, or of policy and systems developed and maintained by government, exposure to the role of leader as facilitator of social change and transformation is needed. In many congregations this training is occurring through clergy experiences of community organizing. Whether through non-profit organizations dedicated to training and deploying church leadership in improving the quality of life in communities that have been disenfranchised, or through alliances developed between religious leaders and labor leaders, clergy are being organized and formed as leaders whose specific role is to organize their religious congregations to be agents for social change in their local communities and beyond.[32] Some seminaries have forged alliances with local organizing groups, providing their students the opportunity to learn about community organizing, which develops leaders utilizing the methodologies of liberative pedagogies.[33] At least one Episcopal diocese now requires community organizer training for its clergy, seeking to equip and form leaders who see their role as providing leadership beyond the church's walls.[34] Clergy leaders equipped in action-reflection as a way to engage and serve the communities to which they are called will facilitate the learning of their congregants. They will identify and develop leaders who have the capacity to problematize and analyze their contexts in order to discern what the Gospel response is to the situations at hand. This pedagogy, applied to the multicultural context, will inevitably lead to more sophisticated conversations regarding race, ethnicity, gender, class, sexual identity and orientation, physical and mental abilities, and access. The ways that these systemic oppressions conflate in diverse communities within pluralistic societies, although at times overwhelming, can lead to identification between groups across lines of difference, forming alliances that organize power to respond and change systems of oppression. This goal of critical multicultural education, to create civic competency for a healthy democracy, is allied with the goal of the Christian community, which in the name of Christ and by the power of the Spirit seeks to transform society so that all can live in just and peaceful communities where life flourishes.

---

[32] There are several organizations that organize religious leaders to become change agents in their community, among them: PICO, IAF (Industrial Areas Foundation), COPS, CLUE (Clergy and Laity United for Economic Justice), and the Gamaliel Foundation.

[33] One such example is Union Theological Seminary, which is collaborating with the leaders of the New Poor People's Movement to provide leadership development committed to social change. See The Poverty Initiative, accessed January 1, 2015, http://www.utsnyc.edu/institues-initiatives/poverty-initiative.

[34] The Episcopal Diocese of Chicago has such a requirement.

CHAPTER SIX

Praxis

The bounded cases of St. Mary's Episcopal Church, Koreatown, Los Angeles and Holy Faith Episcopal Church, Inglewood, provide scenarios in which a liberative pedagogical methodology can be consistently employed in a way that is transformative for the community. The goal of all formation/education in a church context should be to deepen the commitment to discipleship, and to provide opportunities for ongoing growth and exploration of vocation as followers of Christ. The call to faith in the Christian context is a call to discipleship, a call to ongoing learning. The learning described in the gospels, between Jesus and his disciples, is one of engaging the context; acting in healing, reconciling and liberative ways; and then reflecting on these experiences to understand more clearly the ministry to which one is called as a disciple. After encountering a person or situation in need of transformation, whether seen as physical, spiritual, or political, Jesus often sat with the disciples in reflection about what had just transpired. They asked questions, or Jesus asked them questions, and the answers often led to further exploration, as the disciples were invited to continue to minister with him. Through stories/parables, proverbs, questions and challenges, Jesus problematized their understanding of the tradition, always leaving them to reflect further as they continued to engage the context they were called to serve. The sharing of the good news was not primarily achieved through exhortation, but through action and reflection, through modeling and mentoring by the Rabbi, Teacher.

This pedagogy is at work in the vestry meetings, workshops, sermons, and community engagement of both of these cases. The challenge in both cases is to embrace this methodology consistently and intentionally in the formation of leaders for the pluralistic communities they serve. In those instances when another method has been used, to the exclusion of the action reflection model, learning has been limiting, not leading to action and service in an intentional way. The reading of articles and discussing them in the case of St. Mary's Church did not provide culturally appropriate ways of communicating questions, concerns, or doubts. The series of workshops and dialogues offered at Holy Faith provided an opportunity for learning from each other's lived experiences, but ongoing action and reflection would have led to deeper engagement with the differences present, which although named, were not engaged in an ongoing way. Although some members, those participating in the Outreach Commission and later in the Justice and Mercy Commission, continued in action and reflection activities, offering workshops throughout the diocese and participating in actions in support of justice campaigns in Inglewood and Los Angeles, the majority of church members did not. Those members lived with the differences, tolerated the differences, even celebrated the diversity of their community, but they did not engage those differences in a way that might have moved them from mere toleration to a deeper understanding of the intersectionality of oppressive systems operative in their lives, in the congregation, and in society. They did not engage these systems to transform them, and in the process become transformed themselves, where their experiences would lead them to a more empathetic and compassionate response to the challenges faced by fellow church members, in their struggles against injustice. In both of these cases a deeper engagement, sustained over time, would provide the opportunity for greater transformation and growth of the members of the congregation, and of the community as a whole. It would serve as a process of ongoing formation that would inform and be informed by their faith tradition. It would lead to more active engagement with their context, and a more sophisticated analysis of the structural and spiritual transformations required to improve the quality of life of the broader community.

Whether the learning context is a church, community organization, or a public classroom, integrated learning, where topics of difference and justice are studied, must engage conflict respectfully and as a part of the project for liberation. Conflict, not managed, but integrated as a source for understanding the values and beliefs at stake, is an important component in a critical multicultural education process. In *A Powerful Peace: The Integrative*

Thinking Classroom, Heydenberk and Heydenberk offer a framework and strategies for creating a peaceful learning environment. Although their target is classroom contexts, the exercises and processes can be utilized in other contexts, and even the classroom work is intended to have a ripple effect in the broader community. To use conflict in a constructive way to produce communities of peace and justice is a vision of the beloved community that many congregations share.[1] Yet wishing it so, or even affirming that this should be the goal of congregational discussions of difference and conflict, does not make it so. It takes planning, structuring a learning environment that makes this possible, and tools and skills to practice new ways of dealing with conflict when it arises. Understanding and utilizing conflict as a learning opportunity is critical to navigating between and among communities of difference. The term 'integrative learning environment' was inspired by the win-win negotiation strategies, which used the term integrative negotiation for a style characterized by a commitment to "constructive problem solving and conflict resolution."[2] Critical thinking and conflict resolution are integrated to equip students with the life skills necessary to feel competent when issues arise because, contrary to widespread perceptions about the nature of conflict and conflict resolution programs, good programs recognize the need for conflict and enable students to learn from it and use conflict constructively rather becoming its victim. We will never have a conflict free environment: a conflict-positive environment is our goal. Through life skills such as listening, analyzing, brainstorming, and considering multiple perspectives, clear communication develops. Leaders in particular need to be equipped with these skills, especially when they work in a complex and intense context.

In a conflict-positive classroom, cooperative learning enhances appreciation of diversity. The ability to engage competently across lines of difference with tools to manage a difficult or conflict-ridden situation improves relationships and the ability to listen to and learn from one another's experience.[3] Listed below are some of the

---

[1] Warren Heydenberk and Roberta Heydenberk, *A Powerful Peace: The Integrative Thinking Classroom* (Boston: Allyn and Bacon, 2000), xi.
[2] Heydenberk and Heydenberk, *A Powerful Peace*, 2.
[3] Heydenberk and Heydenberk, *A Powerful Peace*, 171.

strategies for addressing conflict presented in the text that could be taught and utilized in a congregational setting.

- ACE paraphrasing: Affirm, Clarify, Express
- Re-quest: reciprocal questioning
- Conflict maps
- "I" statements
- Constructive communication criteria: 3 C's
- Conflict resolution styles
- 3 R's Conflict Resolution: Reset (tone), Restate (paraphrase & clarify), Reframe (define the issue as a problem to be solved, not a win-lose power issue)
- Ground Rules, Guidelines, and Goals
- Cultural Assumptions[4]

There are also church resources that can serve as models for congregations seeking strategies to do ongoing work on issues of justice, cultural differences, and oppression. In the cases presented in *A House of Prayer for All Peoples*,[5] many congregations partnered with community-based organizations dedicated to teaching and empowerment around these issues. Organizations training for community organizing and anti-racist action offer programs that churches can in turn offer their members, to learn and practice living into justice work as a part of their congregational identities. Other resources provide essays and reflection questions; these can be used for ongoing reflection and exploration of possible action that can be taken both within the congregation and in its surrounding community.[6]

Formation occurs through every aspect of community life. The key is to be intentional in what is being communicated, what is being taught. Given the busy schedules of people in congregations it is helpful to provide many different opportunities to participate in reflection and to engage in action. Intentional inclusion of themes of justice, peace, diversity, and pluralism in sermons, retreats, and

---

[4] Heydenberk and Heydenberk, *A Powerful Peace*, 171, 181, 188.
[5] Kujawa-Holbrook, *A House of Prayer for All Peoples*.
[6] A few examples are Spellers', *Radical Welcome* and most of Eric H. F. Law's books, for example, *The Wolf Shall Dwell with the Lamb: A Spirituality for Leadership in a Multicultural Community (St. Louis: Chalice, 1993); The Bush was Blazing but not Consumed* and *Inclusion: Making Room for Grace*.

small group discussions send the message that this is a place where these conversations are welcome. Norms for discussion that emphasize listening for understanding and not for debating can be provided during small group discussions. Invitations to go out and explore their world, and especially the context of their daily lives, for examples of the issues being discussed and for opportunities to address those issues as individuals, as families, and as a community can be issued as part of sermons. Identifying concerns and creating affinity groups to explore them can be the starting point for exploring generative themes with an eye towards possible collective action. What follows is a possible way that these different strategies can be organized into an approximately yearlong project of action-reflection on issues of difference.

A Model for a Year Long Congregational Formation on Issues of Difference Based on a Liberative/Critical Multicultural Pedagogy

Sunday Sermons: The congregation will be invited to reflect on the Sunday sermons at the social hour following the worship services in light of the following questions:

How does our society deal with the issues presented in this morning's sermon?

What are some examples of how society deals with these issues? What does it reveal about society's values and ideals as expressed in their behavior? (These may be different than those that are stated.)

What do we think are the Christian values and ideals regarding the issues raised in today's sermon? What are some examples from the Bible and Church history that express these values and ideals?

What does this mean to us? How do we practice this in our daily lives as Christians in the world?

The questions will be printed in the weekly bulletin so that those who cannot attend the fellowship hour after church will be aware that these discussions are taking place, and they will be encouraged to use these questions in their personal reflection and in discussion with their family and friends during the week. These informal invitations to conversation over coffee after church (and at home) will provide an opportunity for the community to practice reflection together on a regular basis. Many churches struggle with getting people to participate in formal educational forums (Sunday School, Bible Study, Rector's Forums, etc.). Making reflection on spiritual/theological matters a part of the culture of the church by doing it regularly in informal settings will allow the maximum number of people to engage this learning process. These dialogical reflections will engage the majority of the congregation in the first four movements of Groome's liberative education process described earlier in this text.

Creating a climate of reflection is important for creating the expectation of ongoing learning. Most congregations express a concern about children and youth programs, such as Christian Education or Sunday School, but Adult Education is also important, and Christian Formation is a lifelong process. In a discussion on the ideological divide in Adult Education, B. Allan Quigley identifies two histories and delivery systems for Adult Education, the first formal, both in public and community education, and the other informal, lifelong learning.[7] This informal or "non-formal" education and the concrete research concerning it have not been extensively documented but they have a long history in the United States. In secular education the most famous example in the States is the Highlander Research and Education Center in New Market, Tennessee. It is this type of liberative or social reform education that is needed by parishes that are trying to address issues of inclusion and oppression in the church context. The documenting of this type of Christian Education program in urban churches is essential to increasing the knowledge base of Christian Education and Practical Theology and to empowering lay ministers in their ownership of knowledge in these fields.

The preaching and teaching moment on Sundays can be used to present, reflect on, and discuss in brief ways the topics of multiculturalism and inclusion. Although time is limited, doing it in this context will mean that all those who attend worship on Sunday will be part of the conversation and not only those parishioners who choose to participate in a small group discussion or workshop held after church or during the week. It will also set the tone for the reflective work being done; it will make plain that the work is about lifelong learning and formation and not simply about getting some new information so as to be politically correct and non-offensive to

---

[7] B. Allan Quigley, "The Role of Research in the Practice of Adult Education," in *Creating Practical Knowledge Through Action Research: Posing Problems, Solving Problems, and Improving Daily Practice* ed. B. Allan Quigley and Gary W. Kuhne (San Francisco: Jossey-Bass, Spring 1997), 6-7.

the "other people." The work will form the community and define its identity and mission, the people of God, gathered to serve and collaborate with God in the work of redemption, liberation, and reconciliation.

The weekly celebration of the Eucharist, at which all on this journey of faith are welcomed to the table set for all, is a powerful gathering symbol for the diverse community being formed and sustained through its faith. Intentional emphasis on these themes can occur at least once a month. Depending on the setting it may not be possible to do interactive exercises in the pews but what is presented for reflection could take different forms to engage people with different learning styles and interests. The use of the sermon, and reflections on the sermon that can be read and taken home for further consideration, is only one way of presenting material for reflection/discussion. The arts can also be used--presentation of visual, musical, dramatic or literary arts in the form of a Power Point presentation of images on a theme, or poetry, or music presented with lyrics distributed, or a dramatic presentation and other art media can serve as the point of departure for questions. Opportunities for reflection and sharing on the experience of this art and its meaning for each person and how it connects to their personal history and experience can be offered. The advantage of using the arts for presentation of material is that there is material available from many cultures. Exposure to other people's cultural experience will not be limited to listening to someone share about their experience; instead, it will allow people who learn and process information differently to have an opportunity to participate actively in a discussion that does not favor those who find it easy to express themselves verbally about issues that are emotional and visceral as well as intellectual.

Sunday School: At least once a month, the discussion in Sunday School would be directly related to issues of culture, diversity, oppression, and inclusion. In the case of young children this would be through children's stories that come from different cultures and have images and story lines that speak to the diversity of creation. There are many good children's stories that can serve this purpose and that can be connected with a Scripture verse that speaks to the moral/ethical lesson in the story. In addition to the questions presented by the children, the teacher can ask questions that evoke their thoughts about God and community. These "story times" can end with questions about what in the story is the same as in their family and/or community and what is different. For example, the book entitled *The Rainbow Fish* by Marcus Pfister which presents themes of difference, community, and sharing can be paired with a Scripture verse from Genesis 1:31: "God saw all that he had made, and it was very good," (NIV) and children can be asked to name all the different things they like that are good. The sessions can end with a prayer of thanksgiving on the beauty of the God's diverse creation, which can be created by the children with their teacher's help and can be used weekly.

The youth group can have discussions based on the lectionary. The material prepared for the sermons on these topics will be shared with the youth group leader and can be used as content for their discussions. These can also be supplemented with the experiential learning exercises that will be done in the workshops (see below) because it will allow them to debrief as a cultural subgroup and then those who are able to attend the workshops can serve as assistants in the process with the adults.

Vestry: The formal leadership of the church meets regularly as the Vestry. The agenda can begin with a brief reflection on a variety of topics. As part of this yearlong educational program these reflections would be used to do short activities that would allow for discussion on issues of oppression and difference that impact their capacity to live together as a diverse community. This might be as simple as having a fuller discussion of what was presented during the sermon. There might also be ways that the agenda items present an opportunity to discuss how we make decisions or to consider the assumptions operative in the things we choose to do and how we choose to do them. It would also be important for the group to begin to compile the questions that need to be asked when planning or developing a program, activity, event, or group in the church in order to ensure that it is inclusive of the diversity present in their congregation as well as in the community at large. Who is present? Who is not present? To whom would this appeal? Are there ways for people of different ages, or who are fluent in different languages, to participate in this event? What are the cost, transportation, and other access issues? Living as if they are the diverse, inclusive community they seek to become is essential. They cannot wait to be diverse to provide for the needs, expectations, and hopes of people from different communities. Often groups feel they cannot participate in something because it is designed in such a way as to exclude them, however unintentionally. Yet the organizing group doesn't understand why, for example, no elderly or differently abled individuals will attend an event that is held in a location or at a time that would present a challenge to people who have different transportation needs. It is true that, especially given limited resources, the church cannot be all things for all people, but there are many ways to be welcoming and to incorporate diversity that only require flexibility, openness, and thoughtfulness. Being mindful of what those are, naming them, and working towards incorporating these new ways is critical for a community interested in deep diversity and inclusion that goes beyond a cursory sharing of meals and music from different communities.

Workshops: A more intentional and time-intensive experience of learning about cultural diversity is offered through a series of workshops. This series can be offered as a Lenten series or as a special educational program once a month (four to six weekly sessions or once a month for four to six months). In the planning of these workshops, input will be sought from the congregation as to which format would allow for greater participation. Workshops will need to be advertised in various ways for several months in advance to allow people to plan to attend and block out the time. These sessions will be for approximately an hour, and food will be served. Activities will need to be planned for the younger children in order to facilitate the attendance of adults (primarily parents and grandparents). Each workshop session will stand alone so that people can comfortably participate in some sessions if they are not able to commit to attend all of the sessions. The topics of discussion will be advertised with titles that spark interests, preferably relating to stories that have been in the headlines or that are trending in popular culture. One example might be, "What God might say about Princess Boys: a reflection on Gender Identity in Today's Society." In this session the children's book *My Princess Boy* by Cheryl Kilodavis could be read, making this part of the session multigenerational, and the children could then break off to play dress-up or do an arts and crafts activity in which they express people/animals they would like to be. The youth and adults could then continue by seeing the YouTube clip of the interview with the author and her son whose love of all things pink and sparkly inspired the book. The discussion of this topic could be supplemented with a sheet of bible passages that might be relevant (a passage on eunuchs, Paul's proclamation that there is no longer male or female, or Hebrew Scripture passages that speak against cross dressing) with commentary notes.

The issues to be explored will be: class, gender/sexuality, race/ethnicity, and the intersecting and overlapping nature of identity, privileges, and oppressions. It will be important to discuss how all of these categories are social constructions, especially given that social institutions like the church perpetuate these social constructions. Judy Helfand's teaching experience is instructive. In her article "Teaching Outside Whiteness" she describes her classroom discussion, "differences in how we identify do not have to produce social, economic, or cultural difference, I explain, but often categories with which we classify difference (race and gender, for example) are social constructions. They might not exist as categories if they did not support systems that maintain and produce inequality and injustice."[8]

The topic of race will be tackled last because it is for many people in the United States the most challenging and volatile issue of oppression. The discussion of other issues first will allow trust to be built, because the environment created in conversation is not argumentative, but one in which people are all assumed to have knowledge and experience that is important to the group's learning, and that each has lived with some disenfranchisement because of social oppression. This would work well in these congregations where there are no people who are privileged in all categories. The discussion of race and of whiteness in particular will also be sensitive because of the ways it impacts the definition of "Episcopal" identity. The hegemony of whiteness and European cultural assumptions will be challenging for most of the adults for reasons discussed earlier. Boggs' interpretation of Gramsci's definition of hegemony might be instructive here:

> Hegemony combines ideological power with the consent of the people. Gramsci meant the permeation throughout society of an entire system of values, attitudes, beliefs, and morality that has the effect of supporting the status quo in power relations. Hegemony in this sense might be defined as

---

[8] Judy Helfand, "Teaching Outside Whiteness," in *Diversity and Multiculturalism: A Reader*, ed. Shirley R. Steinberg (New York: Peter Lang, 2009), 85.

an 'organizing principle' that is diffused by the process of socialization into every area of daily life. To the extent that this prevailing consciousness is internalized by the population, it becomes part of what is generally called 'common sense' so that the philosophy, culture, and morality of the ruling elite come to appear as the natural order of things.[9]

The issue of cultural hegemony with regards to issues of race and of denominational identity will be challenging for all the members for different reasons. The interdependency of church culture and U.S. white culture is such that it is difficult to define them distinctly. The experience of discussing other issues will at least allow the groundwork to be set for some trust and comfort in the process and its purpose, making it possible to begin to unpack the issues related to white privilege.

These sessions will be formatted roughly the same each time. There will be an opening exercise, reading, or video that will provide the content for the reflective discussion. This will be debriefed with the facilitator providing definitions and important historic and academic considerations relevant to the discussion that can enhance the knowledge and experience being shared.[10] This will be especially important because many of the parishioners are immigrants to the United States and will need information to enhance their understanding of the local context. Participants will be invited to share the ways in which this was expressed in their countries of origin, so as to enrich the conversation with the experiences of oppression and privilege from different contexts. The Episcopal resource for anti-racism training can be used to design these workshops.[11] Finally participants will be encouraged to write in a journal those things that surprised them in their discussion,

[9] Virginia Lea, "Unmasking Whiteness in the Teacher Education College Classroom: Critical and Creative Multicultural Practice," ed. Shirley R. Steinberg, *Diversity and Multiculturalism: A Reader* (New York: Peter Lang, 2009), 62.

[10] For historical materials that reflect an inclusive history of the U.S. see the Zinn Education Project website and explore the teaching materials. https://www.zinnedproject.org/materials

[11] Diversity, Social, and Environmental Ministries Team, Mission Department of the Episcopal Church Center, SEEING THE FACE OF GOD IN EACH OTHER: ANTI-RACISM TRAINING MANUAL OF THE EPISCOPAL CHURCH (New York: The Episcopal Church, 2011).

what impressed them or moved them, and how this might impact their life personally and as a member of the Church. The sessions will end with a closing prayer, possibly the one written by the younger children in Sunday School.

Retreat: Towards the end of this educational project a retreat will be offered for the whole church community where more intense and time-intensive activities can take place. The retreat will open with Morning Prayer using readings, prayers, and songs that reflect the theme of diversity. The retreat will then continue with a series of activities that invite people to share about their identity, their understanding of class, gender/sexuality, and race/ethnicity and the ways these intersect and overlap.[12] In this liberative model the starting point will continue to be their own identities, highlighting that there are many different identities operative in each of our lives. As many activities as possible will be conducted multi-generationally and multi-culturally. Later in the weekend the group will transition to an exploration of how they might do things differently given their reflection on difference, diversity, privilege, and oppression. The retreat will end with small groups brainstorming an activity that would help to share what they have learned with the wider community. These "praxis" plans (the last of Groome's five movements) can be in any arena (politics, the arts, schools, community groups, businesses) and should be doable within a three-month period. The small groups can then come back and discuss the ideas and see what ideas generate the most energy and excitement. These will then be discussed with the congregation at a subsequent vestry meeting to identify ways to implement the project. A general outline of some of the activities and exercises that would be done during the weekend retreat is listed below.

The summer months will provide time and opportunities to develop and implement some of the praxis projects from the retreat, seeking to incorporate all the parishioners and especially those who have participated in the workshops. The intensive, intentional learning will have ended in May, but the goal is to encourage an ongoing process of reflection and action as part of the culture of the church. An annual multicultural celebration can be held to celebrate

---

[12] Resources for activities to learn about issues of oppression are available electronically. For example see, Critical Multicultural Pavilion, accessed January 1, 2015, http://www.edchange.org/multicultural/sites/classroom.html.

and reflect a deeper understanding and appreciation of what it means to be multicultural. The planning of the celebration can also serve as a praxis opportunity, since the planning will now be informed by the learning and sharing that took place. The liturgy and reception will provide an opportunity to share some of the artistic ways that culture was explored through music, drama, visual and literary arts. Having learned from and with each other about the richness of their diversity and the resources it provides for building community, the church will have moved to a place of deeper integration of its identity as an inclusive community.

This project has been presented in general terms because it is my hope that the development and implementation of this program will be done collaboratively with members of the congregation. There are many people with experience in community building, education, activism, and the arts that would enrich the planning and design of this project. As Lea notes, it is part of the hegemonic understanding of education that students are docile recipients of material. To be in dialogue with people exploring the problems faced when our values and understanding conflicts with what is going on in the world around us is what builds "critical, emotional and spiritual literacy."[13] This kind of proposal would be presented to the vestry and others interested in ongoing faith formation around issues of difference. It would be contradictory to advocate for lay leadership as central to the development of inclusive, multicultural, urban churches and then exclude them from the design and planning process. The general skeleton presented here will be enhanced by the participation of the community in the final design. This in itself will be a liberative pedagogy process and will be a form of praxis of exactly the values of inclusion and justice they hope to explore with the wider community.

---

[13] Lea, "Unmasking Whiteness," 66.

Multicultural Exploration Retreat Outline[14]

I: Each day will begin and end with Devotions (Scripture readings, prayers, singing)

II: Ice Breakers:
- *What's in a Name*: Participants share the history of their name (3 minutes each)
- *Personal/Familial Journey to the United States*: The room is used as a map and people move to the locations of origin for previous generations.

Break

III: Rotating Stations of Awareness Activities: Breaking up into smaller groups, each group takes turns at each station participating in the activity and discussion for about 20 minutes each.
- *"Who I am Poems"*: Linking Gender and Sexual Identity
- *The Living Room Scale* ("Weaving the Fabric of Diversity" Unitarian Universalist Association)
- *Race to the Wall*

IV: All group exercise and discussion: Participants will be asked to share their experiences, surprises, affirmations, and understandings from doing the stations.

V: Showing of a movie that explores issues of diversity (for example: "Enough: a Kids Perspective," a film by Zoe Greenberg, or "Scenes from a Parish," a film by James Rutenbeck)

VI: Exercise to prepare for Praxis Brainstorming Groups: "Who is Welcome in Our Congregation?"

VII: Praxis Brainstorming Groups and Plenary to Share Ideas

VIII: Discussion of Next Steps and Evaluation of the Weekend

---

[14] For activities see Critical Multicultural Pavilion accessed January 1, 2015, http://www.edchange.org/multicultural/sites/classroom.html.

Gaps and Questions for Further Study

This present project does not exhaustively present or review materials that have been developed for teaching issues of diversity, oppression, and justice. It presents a theoretical discussion of methodology that would address the needs of leaders of urban congregations in pluralistic communities. It would be helpful to have such a review available to congregational leaders developing workshops for their communities.

A great deal is written about leadership development in various contexts. Styles of leadership, characteristics necessary for successful leadership in changing times, and elements of collaborative leadership are rich topics that should inform the formation and training of leaders in churches in urban, pluralistic contexts. The integration or dialogue with leadership development theory is beyond the scope of this present work but is important work to be explored.

Conclusion

Multicultural Critical Education theory and practice is very applicable in the context of training and developing lay leaders of urban congregations seeking to be transformative agents in their pluralistic contexts. This project has shown why this is critical to Christian formation using the bounded cases of two Episcopal congregations in the Diocese of Los Angeles, St. Mary's Church, Koreatown, Los Angeles and Holy Faith Church, Inglewood. Through their commitment to faithful service while confronting issues of oppression and injustice, we see the challenges of leadership development in their contexts, and the help that a more intentional and ongoing formation process for leaders in highly dynamic communities could be. In times of increased diversification in every community, and a greater awareness of the ways that oppression and cultural differences intersect in Christian congregations, strategies for lay leadership development are critical. This project offers a liberative pedagogy. Many congregations are in this process and their cases provide rich material for future study of best practices in leadership development. Churches can and should be sites of liberative and transformative leadership development, resourcing, supporting, and collaborating with other organizations committed to just, peaceful, and healthy communities. Churches engaged in this challenging and critical work live out concretely their belief that Christ came that all might have life and have it abundantly.

APPENDIX

Reflexivity Journal: Partial Notes Included Here

12/1/14

The census information used to describe the two case studies is not compatible. The categories and tables for a whole city are different than those available for a particular zip code. In the case study on Holy Faith there were categories that are available for a neighborhood in Los Angeles. I had anticipated using the same categories for both case studies, and I will not be able to do that. The descriptions will be slightly different, and this might make the drawing of conclusions less symmetrical.

12/8/14

Struck in the reading done today that I have not been reflecting on my research. This was suggested as an addition to my dissertation proposal, the notes serving to comprise an appendix that would record my experience of the research process itself. I have not done this on a consistent basis that would allow me to date the process of research, and to record immediately, or while still fresh, the insights and the learning that I am gleaning from the process.

It is not insignificant that is in the reading about critical multicultural pedagogy that I am struck with this realization. The omission of the "field notes" was not intentional. I had envisioned the process of collecting these notes with a particular research process in mind, one that was very linear and organized, one that be organized by work days, where I went on site to the congregations and reviewed documents, and wrote notes and then reflected on that day's work. It is not so much that this did not occurs, except for the reflection notes, as it is that the research process was not that clean and uninterrupted. The rushing to go and deal with the quotidian realities of my life meant that the written reflections went undone. This reality leads me to affirm and reaffirm certain realities and challenges faced by the practitioner/activist/practical theologian (and I suspect academic).

In discussion with many others, both people who are from the dominant culture and from "minority" or marginalized cultures, both men and women, I recognize that feeling that somehow one is an imposter as one goes through the process of becoming a scholar is a shared experience. Granted, it is more pronounced and disturbing to women and "minority' or marginalized persons. Probably because this experience participating in an abnormal practice and activity is not limited to academic work. As people constantly defining themselves in contrast to and against a heteronormative, patriarchal, white, middleclass, dominant/hegemonic culture the experience of not fitting in and not being normal is more pervasive. When this feeling is triggered again in the context of academic work it is exacerbated by all the past experiences of feeling out of sorts as one struggles with the right to claim oneself as a member of society, valuable and normal, while reconstructing what is valuable and what is normal. This "imposter" experience, which at its most basic level is about fully incorporating a new role into one's identity and self-understanding, affects the confidence with which one engages the act of research. Inadequacy is a normal experience for those learning something new.

This has been affected further with the current trend in Practical Theology to view qualitative research with human subjects as defining research in the field. My decision to focus on documents as the subject of study seems somehow less academic, or legitimate, or rigorous. I have been grateful for the echoes of my professor, Dr. Greider's discussion of this tendency in practical theology and her hope that this trend does not mean the loss of important research on historic documents and firsthand accounts. It is a little obscene that we would value the words and reflections we collect more highly than those collected by communities themselves, as they seek to document their lives and practices, and as they seek to create and codify their own histories. It is hubris to consider real research only that which we have done, and not what communities have done for themselves. The conversation between the work of academics and the work of communities of practice are what is most necessary, to value the variety of epistemologies, recognizing that the challenges

127

and struggles in which we are engaged cannot afford to dismiss out of hand any knowledge that has been gained in through lived experience, especially not the experience of those most directly engaged and impacted by the injustices and inequities we seek to change in society. But the assumption that my reflection upon my research was not as valuable as "field notes" gathered by the researcher literally in the field with people meant that this aspect of my research process was neglected. I will seek to reconstruct the notes and reflections so as not to miss out on this important aspect of the work I have undertaken.

The importance of the notes has been brought forward in the reading of critical multicultural educators. The reason being that as teachers seeking to both teach and learn from students, the importance of integrating knowledge, reflecting on our own experiences, and noting the places of resistance is central to best practices, especially in critical pedagogies. The reading and discussion of information is not enough to equip teachers or facilitators in working with others to support the development of a critical consciousness. They will file it away as another set of facts to be pulled out and referenced as needed. If indeed the goal of critical multicultural education is to equip people to change unjust structures in society, and if this is being done in a climate that has normalized injustice in such a way that identifying injustice: it's nature, its impact, its roots, is extremely difficult, then we are not seeking to equip persons with a list of handy tools. We are seeking to change the way each of us thinks about society and its impact upon creation in all its forms. That requires ongoing self-reflection, dialogue, critique, and analysis. To do research about this important way of learning, to learn from the writings and experiences of others and not to engage this process myself is to work against my own goal. It is to have lost myself to the system that values knowledge as a commodity outside myself that I must acquire and reproduce in order to achieve recognition as an expert (their knowledge, which I buy via tuition fees and student loans, so that I can become an expert get a job and then pass on, read "bank," that knowledge in others.) I consider myself such an advocate for process, the process of learning and exploring through lived experience and reflection upon that experience and then I submit, through my own academic process which is focused on deadlines and expediency, to a banking and regurgitation model of learning.

Given the fact that I will need to document the ongoing research and writing process, as well as reconstruct the learnings and reflections I failed to document, I will keep these "field" notes/reflections open while reading, writing, rewriting, and editing. I will note what is significant both for me personally as an educator and for the pedagogy I propose for congregational use. In this way I hope to document my own learning process in the preparation of my dissertation and to model and practice the methodology that I propose for congregations and others interested in working with education as a means/medium for social change.

12/10/14

The readings on Foundations of Multicultural Education led me to thoughts about cultural hybridity. The article of Chicana! Riqueña? Need to get my hands on the book that Sheryl recommended about young people and their identities as 2nd, 3rd generation, and the mixture of cultural/racial heritages. At some point we will have to read the work of Foucault, etc. because these are the analyses that people are bringing to the work of cultural analysis. Deconstructing the social symbols and systems at work, especially in identity and culture.

I will also need to deal with the ways that the definitions in the literature on critical multicultural education, anti-racist education and critical multicultural education seem to overlap in terms of the work that I want to do. In the literature from this Foundations text, they make the distinction based on issues and analysis of class. This makes sense in terms of the original source of the work: class analysis being from critical theories. For my take on critical multicultural education, the term critical is more a progressive analysis that takes into account issues of oppression in general in its overlapping areas. Some scholars use the terms in this way, but in this text they are more specific. Will need to do a section on the terms, and the one that is most specific.

December 21-23, 2014 (Time at St. Mary's, Los Angeles)

12/21/14:

I was invited to participate in this service because it was especially multicultural. This Sunday (the 4th Sunday) St. Mary's has a tradition of doing a Christmas Pageant and Christmas Festival.

The service was bilingual, the music multicultural, and instead of the sermon, the children performed the pageant. At the celebration after the mass all of the different cultural groups offered talent for the festivities. The newly named St. Mary's Band, organized by the Oaxacan community played traditional Oaxacan Banda music as well as couple of Christmas carols. A group of beginners played Recorders, whose translation had to be verified by multiple members of the audience, "*Flautas Dulces.*" There was a solo by a young Japanese-American woman, a Mexican Dance by three "mature" women, and a traditional classical Japanese dance by a multicultural/multi-racial group of girls. There was a popular Spanish Christmas song sung by a retired Latino priest, and a Japanese Franciscan Monk Santa Claus, who distributed presents to a diverse group of children of all ages.

There was a great deal of pride by many of the congregational leaders, at the multicultural nature of the celebration, a sign that they had come a long way in their outreach to their neighbors.

12/22/14

The archive room was overwhelming. It was like a time capsule, in process. The archive room is a recently organized project, and there were wonderful story boards of the history of the formation of the community and the experience of World War II, and the internment camps, along with debris, and left over scraps for the organizing of material (old binders, tape, cork boards, bulletins, many pictures). It was clear that all of the material there would be about the history of the parish and would not offer any material about the training process of the congregation, especially not as it relates to the training of leaders for engaging in a multicultural context. Therefore, I decided not to spend a great deal of time in the archive room, instead I reviewed the history boards prepared for the parish's centennial and some articles that are posted in the church office and foyer.

In discussion with the rector (and research fellow, Anna Olson) I was made aware of the lack of documentation about the post internment period. Although there are photographs and journals of the founding of the church, and of the internment period, primarily from historical documents of the period, but there are not documents about the experience of the Japanese and Japanese American community upon their return and their reintegration into life in Los Angeles. The people returned and lived exemplary "American" lives, there were no cultural practices that were traditionally Japanese, they lived lives typical of the late 1940's-1950's. They were members of many religious and civic organizations, and church life was full of activities, bazaars, and church potluck, prominently featuring Jell-O-molds. The trauma of reintegration into a society where it was socially acceptable to discriminate against persons of Japanese descent must have been terrible. Most people did not return to the neighborhoods where they had lived before the forced detainment.

12/23/14

I reviewed the Vestry records for the period from Alix Evans last year at the parish (2008) to the near present (beginning of 2014). Theories of leadership development, formation and management that do not take into account the cultural differences present among leaders can be very problematic. I was struck, sometimes deeply, by the assumptions and comments made about the way that the congregations' leadership operated, specifically communication styles. The assumption that indirect communication is "bad" communication, with no obvious acknowledgement that people of different cultures value different ways of communication, is disrespectful at best, and demeaning at worse. All of the training that is identified in the minutes is without reference to race, culture, class, or any other distinguishing feature to the way that the community organizes its life or lives through its history and experience. The fact that the members of this community seek to blend in with the dominant culture of the Episcopal church as a sign of their integration into mainstream society, their difference already having caused them great suffering and loss, means that they sought to do things as expected by the dominant culture. Having the cultural value they placed on respect, not confronting persons directly in a brash or public manner, labeled "bad," whether recognized or acknowledged, must have been felt.

Some of the communications from the priest to the vestry seem badgering. The constant reminder of the role of the priest in charge, to address conflicts and clarify roles, would seem to indicate that there were concerns or issues related to what the priest thought were behaviors where she was trying to clarify issues and conflicts. But the frequency, several times a year in the two years she served as priest in charge, seems to be in response to resistance or conflict, over the work she was doing in that area. There is no record of any discussion or reflection on the differences of opinion, only a reiteration of the fact that it is the role of the priest in charge to address and resolve conflicts and differences.

This is also noticeable in the various materials that are offered to the vestry for review about various issues they are dealing with. There is an identification of an issue or need that needs to be addressed, then an article or prayer is offered that responds to that issue or conflict (from a particular perspective) and then a moving forward. There are not a variety of ways to view or discuss an issue; there is no notation of a discussion or reflection on the material. It is definitely a banking system of formation at play. The facts, information, and solution is offered by the expert and the students, having received the information, are expected to act on it. The notes of the vestry are sparse in general, so there may have been some questions and discussion, but there are other places in the notes where the fact that discussion occurred is recorded, although the substance of the discussion is not. The fact that these materials are presented and there is no notation of a discussion leaves the questions as to how the material was received, how it was engaged, what questions might have been asked, or if there was simply general assent that this is how "things are done correctly" and then they were followed as prescribed. Yet some of these procedures, articles, job descriptions, were offered multiple times, as if the material was not fully integrated and needed to be re-entered into the proceedings at the meetings and retreats.

On a systems theory note, it is noticeable that each leader of the congregation since the formation of the congregation was identified (anointed/appointed) by the previous leader. The founder of the congregation, Mary Louise Paterson's daughter married the first vicar, their son took over the ministry after his father, the person who had served as his assistant took over the congregation when he left, and the person who served as her assistant took over after her. The priest in charge had been brought in to lead a retreat, and to take over the congregation while the rector was on disability and when she died suddenly that person becomes the priest in charge with no noticeable process (no interviews were recorded, no other names offered and considered. This indicates a very closed system, where current leaders identify future leadership; they have been working under the supervision of the previous leadership, and are mentored and trained in the running of the congregation in this way.

Review and analysis of the Vestry minutes will need to follow, in a simple grid of material presented, and themes identified in the agendas and minutes. This immediate thing that seems to be present, which can be analyzed thematically in detail, and tested, is that much of the work of the vestry was administrative in nature. That is the primary role of the vestry, to deal with temporal aspects of the parish. The management of financial resources, the completion and filing of reports, the authorization of board members and signatures on accounts, the logistics of planning events, are the bulk of the work of the vestry. There is a dearth of information regarding the future direction of the congregation, the vision and hopes of the ministry. When these issues are initially raised, there are no notes as to how to respond and on one of the minutes there is noted a need to spend some time answering these questions, since they are not being answered easily when raised in the congregation. Processes are set up to begin this reflection both by the vestry and the congregation. It is said that the congregation should be brought into the process when the vestry seems unable, unclear, unsure, how to answer the questions regarding the future direction and greater vision of the mission of the congregation.

BIBLIOGRAPHY

Agosto, Efrain. "Paul, Leadership, and the Hispanic Church." In *Seek the Peace of the City: Reflections on Urban Ministry*, by Eldin Villafañe, chap. 10. Grand Rapids: William B. Eerdmans, 1995.

Alban Institute. "Clean Up Bad Communication Habits." May 19, 2008. Accessed January 19, 2015. https://alban.org/archive/cleaning-up-bad-communication-habits/.

Amerson, Philip. *Tell Me City Stories: A Journey for Urban Congregations*. Eugene: Wipf & Stock, 2003.

Archibald, Helen Allen. "Protestant Educators: George A. Coe." Talbot School of Theology. Accessed September 29, 2014. http://www.talbot.edu/ce20/educators/protestant/george_coe/

Bakke, Raymond, and Jim Hart. *The Urban Christian: Effective Ministry in Today's Urban World*. Downers Grove: InterVarsity Press, 1987.

Bakke, Raymond, and Samuel K. Roberts. *The Expanded Mission of 'Old First' Churches*. Valley Forge: Judson, 1986.

Baptist, Willie, and Jan Rehmann. *Pedagogy of the Poor: Building the Movement to End Poverty*. New York: Teachers College Press, 2011.

Barndt, Joseph. *Becoming an Anti-Racist Church: Journeying toward Wholeness*. Minneapolis: Fortress, 2011.

Bass, Dorothy C., and Craig Dykstra, eds. *For Life Abundant: Practical Theology, Theological Education, and Christian Ministry*. Grand Rapids: Wm. B. Eerdmans, 2008.

Bedford, Nancy E. "The Theology of Integral Mission and Community Discernment." In *The Local Church, Agent of Transformation: An Ecclesiology for Integral Mission*, edited Tetsunao Yamamori, and C. Rene Padilla, 99-124. Buenos Aires: Kairos, 2004.

Blumhorst, Roy. *Faithful Rebels, Does the Old-Style Religion Fit the New Style of Life?* Saint Louis: Concordia Publishing House, 1967.

Branson, Mark Lau. *Memories, Hopes, and Conversations: Appreciative Inquiry and Congregational Change*. Herndon, VA: The Alban Institute, 2004.

Branson, Mark Lau, and Juan F. Martinez. *Churches, Cultures and Leadership: A Practical Theology of Congregations and Ethnicities*. Downers Grove, IL: InterVarsity Press, 2011.

Branson and Martinez, *Churches, Cultures and Leadership: A Practical Theology of Congregations and Ethnicities*, second edition. Downers Grove, IL: InterVarsity Press, 2023.

Center for Disease Control Museum. "CDC Museum COVID-19 Timeline." Accessed November 4, 2024. https://www.cdc.gov/museum/timeline/covid19.html

Centinela Hospital Medical Center. "Tommy Lasorda Heart Institute." Accessed September 28, 2014. http://www.centinelamed.com/Our_Services/Tommy_Lasorda_Heart_Institute.html

Christensen, Michael J. *City Streets City People: A Call for Compassion*. Nashville: Abingdon, 1988.

City of Inglewood. "City History." Accessed September 27, 2014. http://www.cityofinglewood.org/about/city_history.asp

City of Inglewood. City Council Minutes. Accessed September 28, 2014. http://www.cityofinglewood.org/city_hall/city_council/min/ccm/2010_minutes.asp

City of Inglewood. "Projects in the Pipeline." Accessed February 24, 2025. https://www.cityofinglewood.org/1499/Projects-in-the-Pipeline

Coe, George A. *A Social Theory of Religious Education*. New York: Charles Scribner's Sons, 1917.

Commins, Gary. *Becoming Bridges: The Spirit and Practice of Diversity*. Cambridge: Cowley Publications, 2007.

Conde-Frazier, Elizabeth, S. Steve Kang, and Gary A. Parrett. *A Many Colored Kingdom: Multicultural Dynamics for Spiritual Formation*. Grand Rapids: Baker Academic, 2004.

Creswell, John W. *Qualitative Inquiry and Research Design: Choosing Among Five Approaches*. Thousand Oaks, CA: Sage Publications, 2007.

Critical Multicultural Pavilion. Accessed January 1, 2015. http://www.edchange.org/multicultural/sites/classroom.html.

Dale, Robert D. *Leadership for a Changing Church: Charting the Shape of the River*. Nashville, TN: Abingdon, 1998.

Darder, Antonia. "Critical Pedagogy, Cultural Democracy, and Biculturalism: The Foundation for a Critical Theory of Bicultural Education." PhD diss., Claremont Graduate University, 1989.

Darling-Hammond, Linda, Jennifer French, and Silvia Paloma Garcia-Lopez. *Learning to Teach for Social Justice*. New York: Teachers College Press, 2002.

135

Data Desk. California's Hospitals Emergency Room Closures. *Los Angeles Times* A Tribune Newspaper website. Accessed September 28, 2014. http://projects.latimes.com/hospitals/emergency-rooms/no/closed/list

Data USA. "Inglewood, CA." Accessed November 4, 2024. https://datausa.io/profile/geo/inglewood-ca/

Data USA. "Los Angeles County (Central--LA City (Central/Koreatown) Puma, CA." Accessed November 4, 2024. https://datausa.io/profile/geo/los-angeles-county-central-la-city-centralkoreatown-puma-ca#:~:text=In%202022%2C%20Los%20Angeles%20County,%2DHispanic)%20(7.82%25),

Davey, Andrew. *Urban Christianity and Global Order: Theological Resources for an Urban Future.* Peabody, Massachusetts: Hendrickson, 2002.

De La Torre, Miguel A. and Gaston Espinosa. *Rethinking Latino(a) Religion and Identity.* Cleveland: Pilgrim, 2006.

Diversity, Social, and Environmental Ministries TEAM, Mission Department of the Episcopal Church Center. SEEING THE FACE OF GOD IN EACH OTHER: ANTI-RACISM TRAINING MANUAL OF THE EPISCOPAL CHURCH. NEW YORK: THE EPISCOPAL CHURCH, 2011.

Duarte, Eduard Manuel, and Stacy Smith. *Foundational Perspectives in Multicultural Education.* New York: Longman, 2000.

Ebaugh, Helen Rose, and Janet Saltzman Chafetz. *Religion and the New Immigrants: Continuities and Adaptation in Immigrant Congregations.* Walnut Creek: AltaMira, 2000.

Elliston, Edgar, J. and J. Timothy Kauffman. *Developing Leaders for Urban Ministries.* New York: Peter Lang, 1993.

The Episcopal Church. *The Book of Common Prayer.* New York: The Church Hymnal Corporation, 1979.

Episcopal Church Foundation. "Who Are We, the Vestry," *The Vestry Resource Guide.* New York: The Episcopal Church Foundation/Cornerstone, 2001.

Episcopal Peace and Justice Network. *White Racial Awareness Process: The Episcopal Church Facilitator Guidelines.* Salem, New Jersey: New Earth, 1993.

Espinoza, Gaston and Virgilio Elizondo, ed. *Latino Religions and Civic Activism in the United States.* New York: Oxford University Press, 2005.

Evans, Alice Frazer, Robert A. Evans, and William Bean Kennedy. *Pedagogies for the Non-Poor.* Maryknoll: Orbis Books, 1987.

Facebook. "LA Riot Boxing." Accessed September 25, 2014. https://www.facebook.com/LARiotBoxing.

Find Law, for Legal Professionals. "U.S. Supreme Court Takao Ozawa v. US, 260 U.S. 178 (1922)." Accessed January 8, 2015. http://caselaw.lp.findlaw.com/cgi-bin/getcase.pl?court=US&vol=260&invol=178.

Find Law for Legal Professionals. "U.S. Supreme Court U.S. v. Bhagat Singh Thind, 261 U.S. 204 (1923)." Accessed January 8, 2015. http://caselaw.lp.findlaw.com/scripts/getcase.pl?navby=CASE&court=US&vol=261&page=204.

Freire, Paulo. *Pedagogy of the Oppressed: 30th Anniversary Edition.* New York: Continuum, 2005.

Geitz, Elizabeth Rankin. *Calling Clergy: A Spiritual and Practical Guide Through the Search Process.* New York: Church Publishing, 2007.

Gillespie, Joanna B. "Japanese-American Episcopalians During World War II: The Congregation of St. Mary's Los Angeles, 1941-1945," Uncovered Voices, Women's 'Pious Memoirs' and Other Mostly Ignored Voices from the Episcopal Church in the 18th and 19th cc. Last modified 2009. http://www.joannabgillespie.com/articleinteredjapanese.html

Giroux, Henry A. *Pedagogy and the Politics of Hope: Theory, Culture, and Schooling.* Boulder, Colorado: Westview, 1997.

Green, Clifford J., ed. *Churches, Cities, and Human Community: Urban Ministry in the United States 1945-1985.* Grand Rapids: Wm. B. Eerdmans, 1996.

Greenway, Roger S., ed. *Discipling the City: A Comprehensive Approach to Urban Ministry.* Eugene: Wipf & Stock, 1997.

Greenway, Roger S., ed. *Guidelines for Urban Church Planting.* Grand Rapids: Baker Book House, 1976.

Groome, Thomas H. *Christian Religious Education: Sharing Our Story and Vision.* San Francisco: HarperCollins, 1981.

Groome, Thomas H. *Sharing Faith: A Comprehensive Approach to Religious Education and Pastoral Ministry: The Way of Shared Praxis.* San Francisco: HarperCollins, 1991.

Harris, Maria. *Fashion Me a People: Curriculum in the Church.* Louisville: Westminster John Knox, 1989.

Hartson, Taylor. "Pandemic Paradoxes: New Patterns of Engagement in a Post-Pandemic World, Observations and Insights from Narrative Responses to the 2022 Parochial Report," Summary of 2022 Episcopal Report Comments. Accessed November 4, 2024. chrome-extension://efaidnbmnnnibpcajpcglclefindmkaj/https://extranet.generalconvention.org/staff/files/download/32270?_gl=1*a0f61r*_ga*MjAzNjY4OTY4My4xNzMwNzM0NzQ2*_ga_8C0Q9J2J2F*MTczMDczNDc0NS4xLjEuMTczMDczMDczNDc2Ny4wLjAuMA.

Heifetz, Ronald, Alexander Grashow, and Marty Linsky. *The Practice of Adaptive Leadership: Tools and Tactics for Changing Your Organization and the World.* Boston: Harvard Business Press, 2009.

Heydenberk, Warren and Roberta Heydenberk. *A Powerful Peace, The Integrative Thinking Classroom.* Boston: Allyn and Bacon, 2000.

Hollywood Park. "History of Hollywood Park." Accessed September 29, 2014. http://hollywoodpark.com/about-history

Holy Faith Episcopal Church, Inglewood. "The Parish Profile of Holy Faith Episcopal Church, Inglewood, CA, May 2002."

hooks, bell. *Teaching Community: A Pedagogy of Hope.* New York: Routledge, 2003.

Inglewood Chamber of Commerce. "Partners for Progress." Accessed September 29, 2014. http://www.inglewoodchamber.com/

Jackson, Bruce W. "Urban Theological Education for Church Leadership." In *Seek the Peace of the City: Reflections on Urban Ministry*, by Eldin Villafañe, chap. 11. Grand Rapids: William B. Eerdmans, 1995.

Jubilee Consortium. Accessed September 27, 2014. http://www.jubileeconsortium.org/about/mission/

Kincheloe, Joe L., and Shirley R. Steinberg. *Changing Multiculturalism.* Buckingham: Open University Press, 1997.

King, Desmond. *Making Americans: Immigration, Race, and the Origins of Diverse Democracy.* Cambridge: Harvard University Press, 2000.

KIWA. Accessed January 20, 2015. http://kiwa.org/.

Kloetzli, Walter, ed. *Challenge and Response in the City: A Theological Consultation on the Urban Church.* Rock Island: Augustana, 1962.

Kloetzli, Walter, and Arthur Hillman. *Urban Church Planning: The Church Discovers Its Community.* Philadelphia: Muhlenberg, 1958.

Kubota, Glenn. "Ascension, Descension." *The PEACE* 7, no. 12, January 1992.

Kujawa-Holbrook, Sheryl. *A House of Prayer for All Peoples: Congregations Building Multiracial Community.* New York: Rowman & Littlefield, 2002.

L.A. Okay, Things to Do in Los Angeles California. "Centinela Adobe." Accessed September 27, 2014. http://www.laokay.com/halac/CentinelaAdobe.htm

Law, Eric H.F. *The Bush was Blazing But Not Consumed.* St. Louis: Chalice, 1996.

Law, Eric H.F. *Holy Currencies: Six Blessings for Sustainable Missional Ministries.* St. Louis: Chalice, 2013.

Law, Eric H.F. *Inclusion: Making Room for Grace.* St. Louis: Chalice, 2000.

Law, Eric H. F. *The Wolf Shall Dwell with the Lamb: A Spirituality for Leadership in a Multicultural Community.* St. Louis: Chalice, 1993.

Le Baron, Michelle and Venashri Pillay. *Conflict Across Cultures: A Unique Experience of Bridging Differences.* Boston: Intercultural, 2006.

Lee, Robert, ed. *Cities and Churches: Readings on the Urban Church.* Philadelphia: Westminster, 1962.

Leiffer, Murray H. *Manual for the Study of the Church.* New York: The Methodist Book Concern, 1939.

Los Angeles Wave Newspaper. "Dotson Padilla Win in Inglewood." Accessed September 20, 2014. http://wavenewspapers.com/news/local/west_edition/article_802f b548-d3c7-11e2-bd4d-001a4bcf6878.html

Massaro, Thomas, S.J. *Living Justice: Catholic Social Teaching in Action.* New York: Rowan & Littlefield, 2011.

Matus, Claudia and Marta Infante. "Undoing Diversity; Knowledge and Neoliberal Discourses in Colleges of Education." *Discourse: Studies in the Cultural Politics of Education* 33 (2011): 293-307.

McKenna, David, ed. *The Urban Crisis: A Symposium on the Racial Problem in the Inner City.* Grand Rapids: Zondervan, 1969.

McManis, Lester W. *Handbook on Christian Education in the Inner City.* New York: Seabury, 1966.

Merriam, Sharan B. *Qualitative Research and Case Study Applications in Education.* San Francisco: Jossey-Bass, 1998.

Meyers, Eleanor Scott, ed. *Envisioning the New City: A Reader on Urban Ministry.* Louisville: Westminster/John Knox, 1992.

Moore, Mary Elizabeth. *Teaching from the Heart: Theology and Educational Method.* Harrisburg, PA: Trinity Press International, 1998.

Neumark, Heidi. *Breathing Space: A Spiritual Journey in the South Bronx.* Boston: Beacon, 2003.

Ngai, Mae M. "The Architecture of Race in American Immigration Law: A Reexamination of the Immigration of Act of 1924." *The Journal of American History* 86, no. 1 (June 1999): 67-92.

Northouse, Peter G. *Leadership: Theory and Practice.* 6th ed. Thousand Oaks, California: SAGE Publications, 2013.

Ormerod, Neil J., and Shane Clifton. *Globalization and the Mission of the Church: Ecclesiological Investigations.* London: T&T Clark, 2009.

Poling, James Newton. *Rethinking Faith: A Constructive Practical Theology.* Minneapolis: Fortress, 2011.

Quigley, B. Allan, and Gary W. Kuhne, eds. *Creating Practical Knowledge Through Action Research: Posing Problems, Solving Problems, and Improving Daily Practice.* San Francisco: Jossey-Bass, 1997.

Ramsden, William E. *Inner Vitality Outward Vigor: The Missional Urban Church.* Mission Resources. New York: General Board of Global Ministries, The United Methodist Church, 1985.

139

Reader, John. *Reconstructing Practical Theology: The Impact of Globalization, Explorations in Practical, Pastoral and Empirical Theology.* Burlington: Ashgate, 2008.

Recinos, Harold. *Hear the Cry: A Latino Pastor Challenges the Church.* Louisville: Westminster/John Knox, 1989.

Rendle, Gilbert R. *Leading Change in the Congregation: Spiritual and Organizational Tools for Leaders.* Durham, North Carolina: Alban Institute Publication, 1998.

Rogers, Donald B., ed. *Urban Church Education.* Birmingham: Religious Education Press, 1989.

Rossatto, Cesar Augusto, Ricky Lee Allen, and Marc Pruyn. *Reinventing Critical Pedagogy: Widening the Circle of Anti-Oppression Education.* New York: Rowman & Littlefield, 2006.

Rothauge, Arlin J. *The Life Cycle in Congregations: A Process of Natural Creation and an Opportunity for New Creation.* New York: Congregational Development Services, The Episcopal Church, 1996.

Rothauge, Arlin J. *Sizing Up A Congregation for New Member Ministry.* New York: The Episcopal Church, Seabury Professional Services, 1984.

Said, Edward W. *Orientalism.* New York: Random House, 1979.

Sassen, Saskia. *Cities in a World Economy: Sociology for a New Century.* Thousand Oaks: Pine Forge, 2006.

Sassen, Saskia. *The Global City: New York, London, Tokyo.* Princeton: Princeton University Press, 2001.

Schaller, Lyle E., ed. *Center City Churches: The New Urban Frontier.* Nashville: Abingdon, 1993.

Schramm-Pate, Susan, and Rhonda B. Jeffries. *Grappling with Diversity: Readings on Civil Rights Pedagogy and Critical Multiculturalism.* New York: State University of New York Press, 2008.

Seale, Clive, Giampietro Gobo, Jaber F. Gubrium, and David Silverman, eds. *Qualitative Research Practice.* Thousand Oaks: Sage Publications, 2010.

Senge, Peter. *The Fifth Discipline: The Art and Practice of the Learning Organization.* New York: Doubleday/Currency, 1990.

The Sentinel. "Inglewood Elections." Accessed September 20, 2014. http://www.lasentinel.net/index.php?option=com_content&view=article&id=10813:inglewood-elections&catid=80&Itemid=170

Slater, Grant. "Boxing Mentor 'The LA Riot' Seeks a Different Kind of Uprising." Southern California Public Radio. Accessed September 20, 2014. http://www.scpr.org/news/2012/04/30/32247/boxing-mentor-who-calls-himself-la-riot-seeks-diff/.

Sleeter, Christine E., and Carl A. Grant. *Making Choices for Multicultural Education: Five Approaches to Race, Class, and Gender.* Hoboken: John Wiley & Sons, 2007.

Sleeter, Christine E. *Multicultural Education as Social Activism.* Albany: State University of New York Press, 1996.

Slessarev-Jamir, Helene. *Prophetic Activism: Progressive Religious Justice Movements in Contemporary America.* New York: New York University Press, 2011.

Solheim, James. "International Reaction to Gene Robinson's Consecration in New Hampshire Mixed." *Anglican Communion News Service.* November 6, 2003. Accessed September 25, 2014. http://www.anglicannews.org/news/2003/11/international-reaction-to-gene-robinsons-consecration-in-new-hampshire-mixed.aspx

Spellers, Stephanie. *Radical Welcome: Embracing God, the Other and the Spirit of Transformation.* New York: Church Publishing, 2006.

St. Mary's Episcopal Church, Los Angeles. "St. Mary's Parish Profile, 2001."

St. Mary's Parish, Los Angeles. "St. Mary's Parish Profile, 2010." Accessed October 2, 2014. http://stmarys-la.org/lang/en/history/parish-profile/

Stake, Robert E. *The Art of Case Study Research.* Thousand Oaks: Sage Publications, 1995.

Steinberg, Shirley, R., ed. *Diversity and Multiculturalism: A Reader.* New York: Peter Lang, 2009.

Stotts, Herbert E. *A Sense of Urgency: An Evaluation of the Urban Workshops.* Urban Pamphlet 5. Philadelphia: The Department of City Work, 1958.

Stumme, Wayne, ed. *The Experience of Hope: Mission and Ministry in Changing Urban Communities.* Minneapolis: Augsburg, 1991.

Swinton, John, and Harriet Mowat. *Practical Theology and Qualitative Research.* London: SCM Press, 2009.

Syemour, Jack L. ed. *Mapping Christian Education: Approaches to Congregational Learning.* Nashville: Abingdon, 1997.

Trulia, "Market Trends." Accessed December 1, 2014. http://www.trulia.com/real_estate/los_angeles-california/market-trends/

UCA News. "Cardijn Taught the Church to See, Judge, Act." Accessed October 1, 2014. http://www.ucanews.com/news/cardijn-taught-the-church-to-see-judge-act/17650

United Methodist Church (U.S.), Council of Bishops. *Urban Church Study.* T.M Pryor, 1975.

The Urban Bishops Coalition. *To Hear and to Heed: The Episcopal Church Listens and Acts in the City.* Cincinnati: Forward Movement Publications, 1978.

U.S. Census Bureau. "American Fact Finder." Accessed September 25, 2014. http://factfinder2.census.gov/faces/nav/jsf/pages/community_facts.xhtml

U. S. Census Bureau. "California Data." Accessed March 2011. http://censtats.census.gov/data/CA/1600636546.pdf

U. S. Census Bureau. "State and County QuickFacts, Inglewood (city), California." Accessed March 20, 2011. http://quickfacts.census.gov/qfd/states/06/0636546.html.

Villafañe, Eldin. *Seek the Peace of the City: Reflections on Urban Ministry.* Grand Rapids: William B. Eerdmans, 1995.

Waddingham, Gladys. *The History of Inglewood.* Inglewood: The Historical Society of Centinela Valley, 1994.

Warner, R. Stephen, ed. *Gatherings in Diaspora: Religious Communities and the New Immigration.* Philadelphia: Temple University Press, 1998.

Weems, Lovett H. Jr. *Church Leadership: Vision, Team, Culture and Integrity.* Nashville: Abingdon, 1993.

Wilkerson, Barbara, ed. *Multicultural Religious Education.* Birmingham: Religious Education Press, 1997.

Windley-Daoust, Jerry. *Living Justice and Peace: Catholic Social Teaching in Practice.* Winona, Minnesota: Saint Mary's Press, 2008.

Wink, Joan. *Critical Pedagogy: Notes from the Real World*, 2nd ed. New York: Longman, 2000.

Wolff, Pierre. *Discernment: The Art of Choosing Well: Based on Ignatian Spirituality.* Ligouri, Missouri: Ligouri/Triumph, 2003.

Yamamori, Tetsunao, and C. Rene Padilla, eds. *The Local Church, Agent of Transformation: An Ecclesiology for Integral Mission.* Buenos Aires: Kairos, 2004.

Ziegenhals, Walter E. *Urban Churches in Transition.* New York: Pilgrim, 1978.

Zinn Education Project. Accessed February 26, 2025. https://www.zinnedproject.org/materials/

www.ingramcontent.com/pod-product-compliance
Lightning Source LLC
LaVergne TN
LVHW052028080426

835513LV00018B/2219

9 781946 230652